ROUTLEDGE LIBRARY EDITIONS: LIBRARY AND INFORMATION SCIENCE

Volume 102

WEEDING OF COLLECTIONS IN SCI-TECH LIBRARIES

WEEDING OF COLLECTIONS IN SCI-TECH LIBRARIES

Edited by
ELLIS MOUNT

LONDON AND NEW YORK

First published in 1986 by The Haworth Press, Inc.

This edition first published in 2020
by Routledge
2 Park Square, Milton Park, Abingdon, Oxon OX14 4RN

and by Routledge
52 Vanderbilt Avenue, New York, NY 10017

Routledge is an imprint of the Taylor & Francis Group, an informa business

© 1986 The Haworth Press, Inc.

All rights reserved. No part of this book may be reprinted or reproduced or utilised in any form or by any electronic, mechanical, or other means, now known or hereafter invented, including photocopying and recording, or in any information storage or retrieval system, without permission in writing from the publishers.

Trademark notice: Product or corporate names may be trademarks or registered trademarks, and are used only for identification and explanation without intent to infringe.

British Library Cataloguing in Publication Data
A catalogue record for this book is available from the British Library

ISBN: 978-0-367-34616-4 (Set)
ISBN: 978-0-429-34352-0 (Set) (ebk)
ISBN: 978-0-367-36248-5 (Volume 102) (hbk)
ISBN: 978-0-429-34490-9 (Volume 102) (ebk)

Publisher's Note
The publisher has gone to great lengths to ensure the quality of this reprint but points out that some imperfections in the original copies may be apparent.

Disclaimer
The publisher has made every effort to trace copyright holders and would welcome correspondence from those they have been unable to trace.

Weeding of Collections in Sci-Tech Libraries

Ellis Mount, Editor

The Haworth Press
New York • London

Weeding of Collections in Sci-Tech Libraries has also been published as *Science & Technology Libraries,* Volume 6, Number 3, Spring 1986.

© 1986 by The Haworth Press, Inc. All rights reserved. No part of this book may be reproduced or utilized in any form or by any means, electronic or mechanical, including photocopying, microfilm and recording, or by any information storage and retrieval system, without permission in writing from the publisher. Printed in the United States of America.

The Haworth Press, Inc., 28 East 22 Street, New York, NY 10010-6194
EUROSPAN/Haworth, 3 Henrietta Street, London, WC2E 8LU England

Library of Congress Cataloging in Publication Data
Main Entry under title:

Weeding of collections in sci-tech libraries.

    Includes bibliographies.
    1. Scientific libraries—Collection development. 2. Technical libraries—Collection development. 3. Discarding of books, periodicals, etc. I. Mount, Ellis.
Z675.T3W43   1986   025.2'1865   85-27010
ISBN 0-86656-552-3

Weeding of Collections in Sci-Tech Libraries

Science & Technology Libraries
Volume 6, Number 3

CONTENTS

Introduction	xi
Weeding in a Corporate Library as Part of a Collection Maintenance Program	1
Richard P. Hulser	
Introduction	1
General Considerations	2
Types of Material	3
Disposal	7
Computer Applications	8
Conclusion	9
Weeding Collections in an Academic Library System: Massachusetts Institute of Technology	11
Jay K. Lucker	
Kate S. Herzog	
Sydney J. Owens	
Weeding Policies	11
Effects of Educational Programs on Weeding	14
Weeding of Engineering Materials	17
Journal Deselection: A Literature Review and an Application	25
Judith A. Segal	
Introduction	25
The Literature Review	26
Evaluation Variables	30
A Case Study and a Deselection Model	34

Journal Weeding in Relation to Declining Faculty Member Publishing — 43
Tony Stankus

Introduction	43
Background	44
Methods	45
How Closely Related Is Age to Cessation of Publication?	45
Arrested Career Development and Cessation of Publication	47
The Wake	47
Negotiating the Cancellation	50
Summary	52

Original Language, Non-English Journals: Weeding Them and Holding Them — 55
Virgil P. Diodato

Introduction	55
The Literature	56
Decision Making Factors	57
Final Comment	64
Appendix	65

Records Management in an Architectural Firm: Skidmore, Owings & Merrill — 69
Catherine R. Burke

Introduction	69
The Collection	70
Operating Procedures	72
Destruction/Weeding of Materials	76
Conclusions/Recommendations	81

SPECIAL PAPER

Science Periodicals in a System-Wide OCLC Conversion Project: Purdue University — 83
Martha J. Bailey

Conversion of Serial Titles	83
Personal Problems	85
Local Errors	89
Conclusion	90

SCI-TECH COLLECTIONS 93
Tony Stankus, Editor

Malnutrition and Disease in the Third World: Sources and Reliability of the Statistics 95
Frank R. Kellerman

Multiple Perspectives and Multiple Problems	95
Sorting Out the Sources	99
Famine's Ongoing Corollary: Selected Diseases of the Third World	105
The Literature	106
Organizations	109
Conclusion	109

NEW REFERENCE WORKS IN SCIENCE AND TECHNOLOGY 113
Robert G. Krupp, Editor

SCI-TECH ONLINE 151
Ellen Nagle, Editor

Database News	151
Search System News	154

SCI-TECH IN REVIEW 159
Suzanne Fedunok, Editor

Foreign Language Barrier	159
Traditional Nonempirical Research	159
Book Selection Using Computers	160
Short Circuits in the Network	161
Bibliographic Instruction for Engineers	161
Online Context of Research	162
User Survey	162
One-Woman Show	163
Searchers Beware	163

Introduction

The process of weeding collections is by no means a recent phenomenon as it undoubtedly dates back to some of the earliest libraries. Many situations call for inauguration of a weeding project, such as lack of space, a desire to place materials in a more suitable library or changing goals of the library. Ideally a policy governs weeding, or deselection, as it is sometimes called.

In this issue the process and the policies for weeding are discussed in different types of libraries. The corporate scene is treated in Richard Hulser's account of weeding in a company library. The academic aspects of weeding are covered in a paper by three librarians at the Massachusetts Institute of Technology, namely Jay Lucker, Kate Herzog and Sydney Owens.

A review of the literature on the weeding of journals plus an application of this process at a university is found in the paper by Judith Segal. A special aspect of journal weeding, its relationship to the publishing records of faculty members, is the subject of the paper by Tony Stankus. Still another special aspect of journal weeding, namely the weeding of original language journals not published in English, is the subject of Virgil Diodato's paper.

The management and weeding of corporate records and drawings at the library of Skidmore, Owings and Merrill, is described in the paper by Catherine Burke.

The special paper for this issue deals with the conversion of entries for serials to AACR2 using OCLC, taking place in the life sciences library at Purdue University, written by Martha Bailey.

The collection specialty for this issue concerns the literature on Third World malnutrition and disease, prepared by Frank Kellerman. Sources for statistics and their reliability are emphasized.

Our regular features make up the remainder of the issue.

Weeding in a Corporate Library as Part of a Collection Maintenance Program

Richard P. Hulser

ABSTRACT. Weeding is an important part of a collection maintenance program. Guidelines are presented for weeding materials in a library which is part of a network of libraries within a company. Factors affecting the weeding of materials such as monographs, serials and internal company reports are explored, along with a discussion concerning some choices available for disposal of these items. This treatment of weeding is based in part on some of the guidelines followed by the staff of the East Fishkill Facility Library of the International Business Machines Corporation. It also includes factors considered by libraries of other companies.

INTRODUCTION

Collection maintenance is a continuing process which includes weeding as an important part. Special libraries in corporate settings weed their collections as much as other libraries. Some corporate libraries are separate entities within a single company. The International Business Machines Corporation's East Fishkill Library is one of more than 40 libraries within its worldwide network of libraries. As a part of such a network, the necessity of weeding materials from the collection, which is housed and maintained for the primary use of employees at the East Fishkill facility, has many factors to be considered. For example, the possible transfer of materials no longer required at one site to be sent to another site is one factor explored as part of a discussion of weeding in a corporate library set-

---

Richard P. Hulser is Senior Librarian of the IBM Corporation General Technology Division Library at the East Fishkill Facility, Hopewell Junction, NY 12533. He holds an MA in Librarianship and Information Management from the University of Denver, an MEd in Instructional Media from Utah State University, and a BS in Earth and Space Sciences from the State University of New York at Stony Brook.

© 1986 by The Haworth Press, Inc. All rights reserved.

ting. The factors presented are not necessarily those in force at the IBM East Fishkill Library but rather a mixture of those used in many different corporate libraries.

GENERAL CONSIDERATIONS

A. Space

Space, or lack of it, tends to be the most visible factor involved with the weeding process. A library has a fixed area of space in which it exists. New materials must be obtained on a regular basis, and room must be made for them.

If materials must be retained, options such as the use of space saving compressed shelving, and/or alternate storage areas away from the main library area can be considered. Such remote storage more often delays the inevitable weeding rather than preventing it. This also contributes to the "out of sight, out of mind" syndrome and the materials become seldom used because they are not readily available. There is also eventual competition for the space with other departments, as well as added administration and control of such a collection.

B. Change of Mission

A change of mission of the people that the library supports occurs over time, sometimes slowly, but usually quickly and repeatedly. This change requires a parallel action in the library so that maintenance and retention of materials no longer relevant to the current work is avoided. However, it is imperative that the librarian and the staff be cognizant of several points:

1. Is the change of mission permanent or is it cyclical? A history of the research/business needs of the company can help in this determination. Although the major mission may have changed, it is possible, perhaps likely, that other work not of current vital importance but important enough to continue on a limited scale, is "put on the back burner". If this is indeed the case, great care must be taken to insure that materials are maintained to support such efforts, not as an extensive collection and weeded as appropriate.

Subject specialists and long-time employees, who are willing, can be of value in tracing the history and business needs of the company.

In addition to available documentation of such information, they become a better resource for the librarian assessing the collection and preparing to weed it.

2. A change of mission for one location within a company such as IBM may often mean that materials should be transferred to a location which has inherited a previous mission of another location. This may preclude a major implementation of other weeding methods. The new location may already have a library and thus the materials are incorporated into the existing collection. If no library exists, which may be the case for a new facility as a result of a company's expansion, the transferred materials become a core for building a collection.

The reverse situation may also occur. Materials may be transferred from one site to another site as a result of a change of mission. In both cases the materials are removed from a library no longer needing them and added to one that does need them. Such intra-library exchange deters purchase of these materials outside the company, especially when some of the materials are most likely out of print and unavailable; therefore, the company saves time and money.

C. *Condition of Materials*

Some materials will begin to fall apart due to repeated use or age. These should be replaced or discarded, as necessary.

These are general considerations for all materials. Attention will now be focused on the types and formats of materials maintained in libraries, including the IBM East Fishkill Library: monographs (including conference proceedings), serials, internal technical reports, and microforms which supplement and/or substitute for the previously named materials.

TYPES OF MATERIAL

A. *Monographs*

A working agreement among a network of libraries within a company can have a provision that a particular library will maintain a complete set of a monograph series or that the library will be a primary source for all monographs (and other materials) which represent subject fields of long-term interest within the company. Keeping within the guidelines of such an agreement helps to refine the weeding process with attention to the following factors:

1. Classics in the fields of research important to the site should be maintained, as well as works of significant authors associated with those areas. In addition, retention of patent information and books which cover the history of the research field and its major events are also important, regardless of the amount of recent use by library customers.
2. Books not fitting within the confines of number 1, and which have not circulated or have not been used within the previous 5 years, are definite candidates for weeding.
3. An effort should be made to contact subject specialists within the company (at your location) for their added advice on retaining books, especially those already noted as strong candidates for weeding.

As part of an effort, during an inventory, to prepare the book collection records (the card catalog) for a changeover from printed form to machine-readable form, a scheme was developed and followed for weeding duplicates from the collection of the East Fishkill Library. The scheme is shown below (keeping in mind the other factors already mentioned):

a. Multiple copies of books which were more than 10 years old were pared to single copies.
b. Books between 5 and 10 years old were weeded to just two copies (when more than two existed).
c. Books less than 5 years old, which existed as multiple copies, were pared to a maximum of three copies for high-use items, and two copies for all others.

The nature of the subject content of the collection as related to major innovations in the subjects represented helped to determine the age boundaries. The result of this careful process was a significant increase in space.

B. *Conference Proceedings*

Conference proceedings are often out of print the day after they are published (if published at all), or soon after initial publication. If a library within a company network has a complete or large run of a particular set of proceedings, it is advantageous to discard a small or incomplete run of that set and borrow from the holding library as necessary. This can only work if the library has agreed to maintain the set and to notify all other libraries if there is an impending need to discard such a set of materials.

C. Serials

Serials often constitute 50% or more of the space requirements of a collection. As a result, weeding is of great importance with these materials. Some serials are published in several parts, as well as several volumes, within one year. One issue can be several inches thick and, as a result, a one-year run of such a title can require storage space of a number of shelves.

Safety is an important consideration which may be overlooked as the result of a space crunch, and this can be a serious mistake. Storage of materials on tops of shelves of ranges can be dangerous to the user as well as the staff. The materials could accidentally fall or the user/staff member could be injured when trying to retrieve an item stored too high. In addition, the materials may block sensors for sprinkler systems for fire prevention or block the sprinklers themselves prohibiting proper and effective operation. For example, fire-dousing water or chemicals could be blocked from covering the maximum area for which they were designed. This is mentioned here, but should also be considered as a precaution for all stored materials.

Keeping in mind these space and safety factors, other points to consider when weeding serials include:

1. If other forms of storage are unavailable, hard copy of full runs of serials should be maintained, as appropriate. Otherwise, keep the current 10 years or other time span of runs, and, for those titles of lasting importance, replace older paper copies with microforms, videodiscs, or other space saving and archival media.
2. A short run of a seldom used title, which may also be relatively old (example: 1958-60), is a strong candidate for weeding. Space gain may not be significant, but eliminating maintenance of this title, reducing staff time devoted to such tasks, may still warrant weeding. This is especially true if another library in the network maintains the same title.

3. Certain titles, due to their general treatment of topics and/or lack of an index or indexing source, are retained by the East Fishkill Library for the current year only. Some are retained for the current year plus one prior year. This time classification helps to weed appropriate older issues on an annual basis. Those titles which are published weekly are maintained in some libraries for as little as 3 months or as long as 2 years, depending upon business needs, space requirements, and availability from other sources.

D. *Internal Technical Reports*

Some corporations, including IBM, maintain microfiche copies of internal technical reports at a central location or the company's headquarters, with distribution to all of its locations as appropriate. A particular location's library sometimes serves as a secondary distribution point for such reports, and therefore retains hard copy of locally produced reports in addition to maintaining a complete microfiche collection of all company reports for local needs. The paper copy of local reports which are part of the corporate collection on microfiche can thus be discarded according to company guidelines.

E. *Microforms*

Microforms often serve as a substitute for hard copy of materials and also serve as supplements to hard copy volumes. An example is the replacement of certain time periods of a serials title, for instance that prior to the current 10 years, from paper copy to microform. Some collections of information are only available on microform, such as a collection of research reports from a major research laboratory or a special technical lecture series, and may also need to be weeded from a particular library's collection of materials. Because of the initial expense in obtaining such a collection, this is often a very difficult decision to make. If the collection can simply be transferred within the company to another library, then such a decision is not so difficult. A transfer through this internal network can offer a nice solution and be cost effective at the same time. It also greatly reduces the need to investigate alternatives such as donation of the materials to agencies outside the company or selling the materials.

Caution should be taken with microform as the alternate storage medium. Customers tend to have an aversion to using it, reproduction quality in paper varies with each vendor's machines, and most importantly, the quality of the images in microform may not be the best. In addition, special illustrations such as diagrams and photographs do not always reproduce well. Color microform is still very expensive and therefore the cost of maintaining paper copy of materials, especially volumes which have important color illustrations, may be more economical than microform.

DISPOSAL

After careful assessment of a collection has been made, various materials are tagged for weeding. The next step is to dispose of them. Disposal of materials in a corporate setting can be subject to internal regulations. Confidential and "Internal Use Only" materials must be handled as defined by the company regulations, while other materials may have to be handled under more general, yet mandatory, guidelines. In addition, the value (or lack of it) of materials to be disposed may be marginal and may not warrant an administrative quagmire in order to eliminate them. The long term effort may be a waste of time and, therefore, certain materials are best just thrown away.

Several options for disposal of materials are as follows:

1. Monographs can be made available to site employees for their work assignments before they are made available to libraries at other locations within the company, are sent to other libraries in the local area outside the company, or are simply thrown away.
2. Serials are often discarded rather than offered to other departments or libraries. Several reasons for such actions are that:
    a. Individual departments have their own subscriptions to the same journal.
    b. An agreement exists within the company's library network to have a particular library maintain a full run of a journal title, with an alert to others in the network if such a run is being considered for disposal, and is therefore not needed by others. (This presents an opportunity for the library to offer its issues to the designated library in order

to replace any missing issues or gaps in the run.) In addition, other libraries within the network may discard all issues of that title prior to a certain time period and therefore may not need the issues (due to lack of long term value, etc.).
- c. The physical condition of the issues is so poor as to make them unrepairable and almost useless.
- d. Some titles are so specialized that local libraries have no use for them, and the administrative effort to seek other libraries who may want them is both time consuming and expensive to warrant such a search. This is particularly true for libraries where there is a small staff who must also carry on daily activities without interruption.

Serials may not be weeded, on the other hand, based on factors such as:
- a. They contain papers written by people at your location.
- b. Photocopy requests and/or active use of particular titles.
- c. Impact factor or usefulness of the contents over time.

3. There are used periodical dealers who pay cost per pound and will haul discards away for you. Other dealers exist who will buy books or sets of books. This kind of disposal can be complex and should be coordinated through the proper offices within the company so that all internal regulations are followed with the proper authorizations.

COMPUTER APPLICATIONS

The use of computers in a library is not new, however, the current widespread availability of such technology at a reasonable cost to a small operation such as a company library is new. In addition, development of applications such as tracking materials for potential weeding or designating them for binding have been made possible on a local level only recently.

An IBM Personal Computer is used to reduce administrative work in the East Fishkill Library office. One of the parts of a serials module, developed using a data base management software package, enables the titles to be discarded to be tagged so that the computer can generate a "discard list". This makes the chore of compiling such lists relatively simple. The titles marked as current year only, etc., can also be listed in order to aid in annual weeding and also to aid with determining the titles to be bound.

CONCLUSION

With careful thought and planning, weeding in a corporate library setting can be accomplished using the guidelines outlined here, as well as those which are standard for all types of libraries. Slote[1] gives an extensive treatment to weeding in his book. More specific applications to special libraries are discussed in a chapter on weeding materials by Mount[2] in his text.

Utilization of a network of libraries within a company on a cooperative basis can enhance the weeding process and keep resources available "in-house" as needed.

REFERENCES

1. Slote, Stanley J. *Weeding library collections—II*. 2nd rev. ed. Littleton, CO: Libraries Unlimited; 1982.
2. Mount, Ellis. *Special libraries and information centers: an introductory text*. New York: Special Libraries Association; 1983: Chapter 21.

Weeding Collections in an Academic Library System: Massachusetts Institute of Technology

Jay K. Lucker
Kate S. Herzog
Sydney J. Owens

ABSTRACT. Begins with a review of the policies that govern the weeding of collections in the MIT library system, particularly the conservation of space, the need to keep abreast of changing educational programs and the need to reinstate collections as programs return to activity. The preparation of budgets to accomplish these goals and the deselection process are described, followed by a discussion of the actual weeding process in terms of different types of materials, such as monographs, serials, technical reports, government documents and society-sponsored papers.

WEEDING POLICIES

While most research library administrators would support the desirability and even the necessity for developing and implementing weeding programs, the carrying out of such a policy is often relegated to a priority level that guarantees little progress. Although libraries would profess to support the concept of dynamic, well-managed, and institutionally-relevant collections, it is often the more mundane but irresistible force of the lack of space that provides the

---

Jay K. Lucker is Director of Libraries, MIT, Cambridge, MA 02139. He has an AB degree from Brooklyn College and an MS from Columbia University School of Library Service. Kate S. Herzog is Associate Engineering Librarian and Collections Manager of MIT Engineering Libraries. She has an AB degree from Vassar College, the MAT degree from the Harvard University School of Education and the MS degree from Simmons College School of Library and Information Science. Sydney J. Owens is Associate Science Librarian and Collections Manager of MIT Science Libraries. She has an AB degree from Bryn Mawr College (chemistry) and the MS degree from Simmons College School of Library and Information Science.

© 1986 by The Haworth Press, Inc. All rights reserved.

necessary momentum. At MIT, there has been a long history of collection weeding, although it was not until the last decade that an overall institutional policy began to be formulated. Over the years, MIT has led the ARL libraries statistically in the proportion of volumes discarded to volumes added. While some of this can be attributed to what may be the idiosyncratic policy of counting multiple copies acquired for reserve only to see them withdrawn a few years later, MIT has been withdrawing unique materials from the collections for many years. More will be said later in this article about what types of material are candidates for pruning from the collections.

The philosophy that drives the MIT Libraries collection policy as it relates to weeding is closely connected to the rather special nature of MIT as a research university polarized around science and engineering. Some of the factors that need to be understood in looking at collection management at MIT are the following:

- About 60% of the students, graduate and undergraduate, are in the School of Engineering.
- About 85% of all teaching and research is in science and engineering.
- There are however, strong teaching and research programs in architecture and planning, in economics, political science and management, and in linguistics, philosophy, and cognitive science.
- Other than the disciplines mentioned above, there are no research or graduate teaching programs in the traditional humanities, i.e., history, literature, foreign languages, music, anthropology, archaeology, *but* undergraduate courses are taught in all of these areas.
- The predominant interest of the majority of users, especially in science and engineering, is in the most recently published information, with periodical literature dominating.
- There are, however, substantial numbers of students and faculty interested in the historical aspects of a number of fields, particularly technology, architecture, and science.
- The MIT Libraries is a decentralized group of subject collections with no single, central library.
- Space is at a premium and may be more difficult to obtain than money although securing reasonable guarantees of the latter occupies much of the Director of Libraries' attention.

- While there are constant changes in research directions and emphasis, and while new fields of interest arise with total unpredictability, the university has tended to maintain a fairly stable proportion of its activities distributed among the various disciplines.
- On the other hand, it is never safe to assume that an area in relative decline will stay that way forever. An example is mining and mineral resources that was relatively dormant for almost 15 years before being revived in the mid-1970's.

The three factors that have the most pronounced impact upon the contents of the active collections in the MIT Libraries are, in order of importance, space, intellectual relevance, and long-term value. Space is clearly the predominant factor in that the MIT Libraries are in essentially a "zero-growth on campus" situation. For a number of years the libraries have had to remove from active collections and either transfer to storage or discard an amount of material roughly equal to that acquired. There is no reason to suspect that this situation will change significantly in the foreseeable future although there is some hope that additional space may be found for the Architecture and Planning Library, the most crowded of all collections.

What is kept, for how long, and where, are the principal questions that drive the development of a weeding philosophy for the MIT Libraries. In addition to the institutional factors described above, there are a number of other issues that influence both macro- and micro-strategy. One of the most essential aspects of the MIT collection management program is the need for reversibility. Obviously, once an item is withdrawn from the collections, the reversing of that process is both difficult and expensive. Relegation to storage, therefore, is a much more sensible route and is the one that is followed for the vast majority of cases. At present, approximately 20% of the total printed collection of the MIT Libraries is in storage. Almost all of that is in a facility located on the perimeter of the campus. Material is delivered to and from this facility twice per day with a guarantee of 24-hour delivery anywhere on campus.

In the broadest terms, the MIT Libraries are committed to maintain research level collections in fields of traditional (historical) strength and current interest. These two, however, are not synonymous. While the history of technology has long been a strong collecting interest of the libraries this discipline only recently revived from a number of years of inactivity with the establishment in the late 1970's of a Program in Science, Technology, and Society. There is no question that MIT will continue to acquire and maintain strong research level collections in engineering, science, architecture and planning management, economics, political science, linguistics, philosophy, and cognitive science. Indeed, a number of these fields are areas in which MIT has proposed its collections be designated for priority in the national retrospective conversion program of the Association of Research Libraries.

One factor motivating the weeding of materials, principally from the active libraries to storage, has a strong influence in at least one of our divisional libraries. That is the matter of changing theories and what some of the faculty have identified as "wrong science". There are some individuals especially, but not exclusively, in biology, who feel that "leaving" older books with incorrect information on the shelves of active collections is a disservice to users, particularly students. The pros and cons of that argument might well be the text for a further article on weeding.

In general, MIT would prefer to keep unique materials rather than withdraw them. The rationale for such a philosophy is that it costs more to withdraw than to store, at least in the short run. Present estimates are that it costs between $5 and $7 per file to withdraw an item but it costs between $.05 and $.10 per year to store a volume. While the long term economics seem to favor storage it is also evident that if one weeds, one can get much more cost effectiveness weeding serials than weeding monographs.

The MIT philosophy of weeding may in summary be characterized as evolving, dynamic, institutionally-relevant, and space-driven. It is affected by (1) MIT's responsibility as part of the national community of research libraries; (2) local consortial responsibilities as a member of the Boston Library Consortium; (3) current, anticipated, and prospective needs of the institutional community.

EFFECTS OF EDUCATIONAL PROGRAMS ON WEEDING

Knowledge of an institution's research and educational program is particularly important when making weeding or deselection decisions. This is especially true at MIT with its high volume of external support for research, including thesis and dissertation work. MIT's collection management program emphasizes a program-centered approach based on an understanding of current research and educational focus.

MIT consists of not only traditional academic departments but also an unusually high number of interdisciplinary centers (Cancer Research Center, Clinical Research Center of the Nutrition and Food Science Department), and special focus laboratories (Research Laboratory for Electronics, National Magnet Laboratory). These centers typically develop on an ad hoc basis, growing from mutual research interests of existing staff, who then seek external sources of funding support for their projects, hire additional staff and pursue targeted or mission-oriented research.

Funding and staffing of these centers and labs waxes and wanes but the centers rarely actually dissolve or close. Contract and grant funding provides work for students from the bachelor's to the doctoral level which increases the size of some centers. MIT emphasizes opportunities for research involvement beginning at the Bachelor's level with a program entitled Undergraduate Research Opportunities, which also provides financial support. Since a very high percentage of the faculty, staff and students are thus involved in externally supported research in addition to the educational mission of the university, it becomes especially important for the libraries to have information about the size and current status of various research programs.

Measures of program scope are available from various sources.[1] The registrar's report details enrollment by level of student and specific course, gives number of graduate and undergraduates by department and school, and shows the faculty, staff, and sponsored research staff and their affiliations. Individual course offerings can be assigned to subject lines across traditional library boundaries. A course taught in the Civil Engineering Department which chiefly concerns stream ecology and groundwater biology and chemistry can be assigned to the Biology or Environment lines in the appropriate library, not necessarily to the Engineering Library budget. Faculty curriculum vitae are a good source of the research interests faculty carry with them to a new institution, and of preferred journals in which they publish.

The treasurer's report gives broad financial information and a more specialized report of sponsored research details grant and contract topic, principal investigator and amount of funding. An analysis of this information can lead to some surprises: for example, 30% of MIT's total research volume is attributed to biomedical research, which does not fit the stereotyped idea of MIT's interests. Close examiniation of the available program information is important for precisely that reason, and prevents collections which are built on out-of-date assumptions about needs.

Program budgets can then be constructed using this and any other available institutional information. There is of course not a direct proportion between the number of students or researchers and the budget allocation. Factors such as the serial-intensive nature of some subject areas and the importance of historical sources and need for retrospective purchases also influence the budget. There are differences in costs of supporting dissertation research not only between the Humanities and the Sciences but also from one Science discipline to another. Economies of scale are also in force in some disciplines; the library needs of an MBA candidate are quite different from an MS candidate in science, for example.

Program budgets in the MIT libraries are thus organized by focus of program, by research effort, or by academic disciplines. Examples of budget lines could be Energy or perhaps Biotechnology, which incorporates aspects of chemical engineering, molecular biology, and biochemistry.

When "mission-oriented" or special focus programs develop statistical information mentioned above this is useful in requesting money for library support for new programs or for significant changes in focus or for reallocating funds from traditional areas to emerging research interests.

When funding and/or interest declines in an area such as energy research the information collected when the program was growing can be used to analyze the decline of the program. It is usually not the case that all research grants are terminated, but some specifically targeted work remains. It is important to continue to acquire materials which are needed to support this work and to suspend purchasing in these areas which are no longer active. Only detailed information about sources and types of funding can provide the basis for such decisions.

Once available information about contract research and dissertation research and other educational programs has been gathered and analyzed, reallocations in monograph funds and periodicals subscriptions can be made. Monograph accounts can be more readily changed in direction than can periodical accounts. The increasingly interdisciplinary nature of science means that individual periodical titles are of interest to researchers in many fields, and it grows more difficult to identify potential subscriptions to tie to decreased research funding. Program budgeting for both monographs and periodicals makes this task easier. Once candidates for cancellation have been identified faculty liaison are very useful in reviewing the selection of titles. Another check on the actual use of periodicals in specific disciplines is a review of citations in theses in that area. This separates the wishful thinking of titles it would be nice to have from those titles which are actually relevant and relied upon.

Mosher[2] stresses the importance of using more than one criterion or method in identifying material for deselection and advises that a mechanical technique such as use studies or citation frequency be used in addition to the judgmental considerations of program needs. When the driving force in deselection is decreased funding or program changes, a check against errors is to consider the periodical "suspended" and to retain the back files until it is certain that the research program that title supported is not simply undergoing politically-engendered vicissitudes of fortune. Monograph weeding down to a single copy of a title can be supported, but wholesale weeding of monograph collections must be done with care lest interest in that area revive after a short hiatus. An example of this at MIT is health planning which was studied in the School of Architecture and Planning until about five years ago and now is being revived in the Sloan School of Management and in the Whitaker College of Health Science, Technology, and Management.

When deselection decisions have been made based on a knowledge of institutional program changes, there may be a greater degree of confidence about what is always a difficult decision.

WEEDING OF ENGINEERING MATERIALS

When dealing with weeding, the collections manager must balance several cost factors: the costs of acquisition, of cataloging, and of retaining the material. Acquisition includes selection, searching and ordering and receipt processing. The cost of cataloging varies depending on whether copy cataloging can be done or original cataloging is required. The cost of retention is related to the useful lifespan of the material, space needs in live storage, space availability in remote storage and staff costs in reviewing materials and in deaccessioning or reprocessing them for a remote location. Different materials lend themselves to different storage/withdrawal patterns.

The selector makes a "weeding" decision every time he/she chooses not to buy a monograph. But often the cost of cataloging a book is equal to or greater than the cost of acquiring it. In that case, a system which allows for review after receipt and before cataloging may be useful.

At MIT, the "precataloged book" system was initiated to make books accessible to the users by placing them on the libraries' shelves prior to their being cataloged. When materials are received, they are searched on OCLC. If LC copy is found, they are cataloged by copy catalogers before being sent to the ordering library. Those materials for which there is no LC copy are sent to the ordering library to be shelved by order number and enter a "hold" period of at least six months before being recalled for cataloging. This system is beneficial, not only for the Catalog Department, but also for the collections development process. It allows the subject specialist to "review" materials upon receipt and before cataloging. At that time, the decision might be made to withdraw the book immediately (if its scope and level aren't suitable) and to offer it to another library in the system if appropriate; to review the use and content prior to returning the item for cataloging (if its level is marginal or if it's one of many texts on the same subject); or to put the monograph on a priority list to ensure that it be cataloged as soon as possible.

The above method works for monograph review as titles are being added to the collection. Usually, the need is to weed an existing monograph collection. Since this must be done either on a title-by-title review basis or by moving entire collections from active locations to storage, such monograph reviews are by their nature large collections projects. Obvious candidates for storage are older Dewey decimal classed collections. When a system makes the decision to store such collections, provision should be made to allow for the reclassification of materials which receive significant use so they can be reincorporated into the active collection. Current serial titles would also require reclassification from Dewey. Moving a whole LC class range out of active stacks and into storage, while being easy to do physically and easier for the user to understand intellectually, raises problems for users when there are newer materials which they require out of storage. An automated circulation system should provide the library with a list of lesser-used titles to review for possible relegation to storage. If this method is chosen, the library's procedures should be simple enough to allow for the easy transferring of materials from active to remote locations and back again, since use patterns do change over time and so should storage decisions.

By far the most expensive materials added to any library's collection are serials. In addition to the cost of the subscription, there are the costs of check-in, binding, cataloging, shelving individual pieces as they are received as well as the cost of the shelf-space occupied by the title. Even if a library has a policy of requesting a sample issue, rather than ordering from publisher's blurbs, the selector will find that occasionally the title which is received is not what it was touted to be. Therefore, a system which has built-in review for new serial and journal titles, while it is an added step in the acquisition process, will ultimately allow for more coordinated control of collection growth.

At the Barker Engineering Library, we have established a systematic, on-going review of our serial titles as follows:

1. Review upon receipt. At that time a retention/binding decision is made. If the title is known to be a scholarly one which must be retained, no matter what happens in its published life, the binding decision is made; and the title will not need subsequent review. Also at that time, a trade publication which will have limited long-term value but high short-term interest might be assigned a limited holdings statement in lieu of a binding decision. Usually, however, the selector will want to wait a year or two to see how the title develops and to assess both its content and its use. In those cases, the decision will be to attach use labels to the issues as they are checked-in and to review the title after the appropriate time has passed.
2. Titles which were identified for review after they had been held as above are sent directly to the subject specialist in the month/year which was first designated. Then the selector can assess subscription cost, use, usefulness and compare the title to others which may be even better and which were acquired since the first subscription was placed. This is an appropriate time to consider not only binding, but also the advisability of substituting microform for retention if the issues being reviewed have been heavily used and/or damaged.
3. Whenever a title changes, the title is reviewed again to see if there are any changes in content, format, or intended audience which have rendered the new title inappropriate for the library's collection. Here, the application of a precataloging

system is also beneficial, since retention decisions are best made prior to the investment in cataloging.
4. When a title ceases publication or merges with another title, it is reviewed again from both the perspective of retention and of storage (either now or at some later date, when the use of the material will have dropped-off).
5. If the subscription price increases by n%, the collection manager might want to review the title to see if use and content still justify the money being spent to acquire the title.

The above cases are applied for all titles in Barker, but can be limited to those which do not come from the library's major societies. The reason we look at all new titles in Barker is to ensure that duplicate paper copy or microfiche subscriptions are placed for heavily-used society publications.

Additional reviews take place periodically as a result of system-wide decisions. Several reviews of duplicate subscriptions have taken place at MIT over the past fifteen years, either to substantially reduce serials commitments or to reduce the level of duplication among libraries with which we have cooperative agreements.

There are several ways in which a library can try to maintain a steady-state serials collection. In addition to reviewing retention as outlined above, the library can designate a certain cut-off date before which journals are kept in storage. For serials, a unilateral cut-off date is less reliable. A review of serials title-by-title on the shelf will indicate a point which would be appropriate for storage of a given title. In that case, the holdings policy can be established: keep n years of the title in the live collection and all earlier years in storage. Using this system, every time a new year is received, the corresponding earlier year is automatically "bumped" into the storage collection. Of course, the use of microform either in lieu of or in addition to paper copy retention is an option which the collection manager must always consider. For serials which provide statistical data, we have found that a "five-year formula" meets our users needs. The formula retains every fifth year of the title as well as the latest five years.

The easiest class of material to "weed" is an uncataloged collection. Despite the cost of obtaining these materials, the lower the cost of initial processing into this collection, the lower the cost of withdrawing these same items will be. Technical reports fall into this category. Ignoring technical reports collections which should be retained to fulfill depository agreements (like NACA/NASA or AEC/ERDA/DOE collections), there are large non-deposit collections of reports which have been built by obtaining individual gifts or received on exchange, on a mailing list, or on subscription from a variety of sources. Even if a library's policy is to discard paper copy technical reports if they are duplicated in microfiche or to retain only microfiche technical report collections, most libraries do not have the space required to store ever-growing microfiche collections.

At the Barker Engineering Library, we have noticed that as the number of technical reports has increased their use has drastically fallen off. In addition, no matter how carefully one tries to select technical reports which should be valuable (either by the NTIS SRIM profile or by selection of individual reports to be ordered), the reference librarian can attest to the number of reports which users seek as a result of online searches (or other people's bibliographies) and do not find in the library's collection. Given such a low satisfaction ratio, a more limited collection pattern for technical reports is justified.

While developing a weeding policy for technical reports, the collection manager must consider the relative importance of this format to specific subject literatures. For instance, use of technical reports is higher in aeronautics and ocean engineering than in electrical and mechanical engineering. Another factor to be considered is the ease by which individual reports can be obtained if a user requests one. While a foreign report might take weeks to verify and order, an NTIS report can be rushed for a user in a matter of days. A critical element in weeding technical reports is the definition of series which are "essential" to an engineering collection. In each field, there are certain series or report issuing agencies which have stood the test of time. And, if the library has chosen to treat them as technical reports, rather than as open-entry serials, these series should be retained in full, even if other reports are being kept for a more limited time period.

In theory, a "steady state" technical reports collection might keep as "latest n years only" reports received on NTIS SRIM and to retain only reports in selected series (like Stanford Artificial Intelligence Memos or David W. Taylor Naval Ship Research and Development Center reports). This weeding procedure is aided by the fact that, following the lead of NASA, DOE and PB reports now include digits for publication years in their accession numbers. In practice, an added factor in the weeding policy might be to examine pieces for "use" prior to discarding them. If use criteria are met, a piece might be retained for more than the n-year period.

Another large collection which is usually uncataloged, costs little to acquire but more to process, and is coming increasingly in microform, is government documents. Unless a library is a regional depository, it will probably not want to retain uncataloged government documents for more than five years. The problem involved in maintaining a "steady state" here is to easily identify pieces which are more than five years old and can be weeded. A simple data file system input on your library's personal computer can not only answer the question "does your library have this document?" but can also generate lists of items which are discardable on a certain date. However, the proliferation of new offerings prevents the five-year retention from controlling collection growth. Therefore, at MIT we routinely review new government documents as they are received, not only to ensure that important ones are cataloged appropriately, but also to monitor the content of pieces being received on a given item number. If we find that the content of an item is not relevant, we cancel the selection of that item number.

Society papers are a good example of the variety in professional organizations' microform awareness. The Society of Manufacturing Engineers (SME) has for years been providing simultaneous fiche subscriptions to engineering libraries. The American Institute of Aeronautics and Astronautics (AIAA) provides fiche on a delay basis (usually a month or more) once the paper has been indexed and accessioned by their Technical Information Service for *International Aerospace Abstracts*. The Society of Automotive Engineers (SAE) makes the entire year's worth of papers available at one time (at least half a year into the following year). Other organizations, like the Society of Petroleum Engineers (SPE), provide similar annual sets through University Microfilms. And some, like the American Society of Mechanical Engineers (ASME), provide only paper copy.

By their own policies, these organizations effect selection/retention policies for their papers in libraries. Where fiche are simultaneously available, fiche is the obvious choice. When there is a delay, the patron demand for the newest papers as well as the library's budget are controlling factors in whether to purchase a duplicate set on fiche and discard the paper copy (as Barker does for the SAE), whether to purchase the paper copy only (AIAA), or whether to decline the purchase of paper copy to wait to buy the microfiche when it becomes available (SPE).

REFERENCES

1. American Library Association. *Guidelines for collection development,* Chicago; 1979.
2. Mosher, Paul, Managing library collections: the process of review and screening. In: Steuart, Robert, et al., eds. *Collection development in libraries: a treatise.* Greenwich, CT; Jai Press; 1980; p. 159-180.

Journal Deselection:
A Literature Review
and an Application

Judith A. Segal

INTRODUCTION

Difficult as it is to choose which published materials to purchase with limited funds, it is even more difficult to decide which to discard, or, as in the case of periodicals, which to discontinue. Terminology is often very revealing of attitudes and in this process the library profession alternates in using the terms "deselection" and "weeding." Deselection implies undoing a past action, one of selecting. In both cases a modicum of choice is involved. On the other hand, weeding implies ridding an area of the undesirable, even infectious. Forced to cut back on expenses, libraries have to learn the wisest and most economical ways to maintain their aims and goals and yet stay afloat on an appropriated budget. In choosing to discontinue journals, they may feel regret and anxiety rather than victory over a nuisance. Throughout this review, the term "deselection" will be used.

As each candidate journal steps forward for a deselection review, the multitude of factors considered important never seem to group themselves consistently under one title. In science and technology libraries the need for current information is amongst the most crucial factors, but even here problems arise. For example, a particular journal is used rarely, but it appears on no union list and is unlikely to be available if desired through interlibrary loan. Another is rather inexpensive and has a faithful following of 2-3 faculty members, unlike a newly requested expensive current information

---

Judith Segal is a Senior Reference Librarian at the Ben Gurion University of the Negev in Beersheva, Israel. She is currently on an extended leave as a Teaching Assistant in the doctoral program of Columbia University's School of Library Service, New York, NY 10027.

© 1986 by The Haworth Press, Inc. All rights reserved.

title by a department promising 15 faithful readers, yet not ordered because of a library policy of one purchase per cancellation. The list of problematics in decision making could go on and on, but the time for decision making and the funds available are not as flexible. Many a library stands at the edge of a higher committee's patience and must trim the budget 10-15-20% or else!

This review has been written, therefore, to bring together the published theory and practice in the area of deselection of journals in order to assist librarians in their own policy decisions and tactics with regard to journal deselection. Much as it is an unpleasant duty, it is more and more forced upon libraries by uncontrollable inflation and impoverished budgets unable to maintain their former purchasing power. Following the literature review will be a case study of the author's periodicals deselection project in Ben Gurion University of the Negev, Beersheva, Israel.

A literature search revealed some 53 articles and monographs since 1976 on the subject of journal deselection in the academic, research and special library, the subjects of this study. As opposed to school and public libraries, the above were chosen because they are most likely to have special collections such as Science and Technology and special clientele—faculty, researchers and graduate students—who feel comfortable and capable of participating in the deselection decision-making process. The year 1976 was chosen as the cut-off point because it appears to be the time when libraries were becoming very much aware of the anomalies of journal economics. Although all 53 sources were examined, only those most inclusive of theory and practice, dealing with either the issues and criteria behind journal deselection or that and a specific application, have been selected for discussion. Furthermore citations specifically and solely discussing journal obsolescence, relegation to storage, and format transformation (i.e., hard copy to microform), have not been reviewed.

THE LITERATURE REVIEW

It is said that there are about 100,000 extant journals and that that figure is likely to reach one million by the early 21st century.[1,2] The massive output and concurrent pressure to acquire collided with the enormous inflationary spiral of the 70's. Johnson claimed that in that one decade of the 70's, "prices for domestic books rose by 273%, while prices for periodicals rose 398%".[3] It was, as Bobinski claimed, the end of the Library Golden Age.[4] Uncontrollable publication and simultaneous run-away purchase prices of books and journals both were greatly outdistancing shrunken budgets. Appropriation increases for libraries even fell behind the general budget increases of their controlling institutions.[5] As a result, traditional library acquisitions operations were changing more by fate than by thoughtful policy reconsideration. Since journals were high in demand as well as cost, their acquisition was taking priority over that of monographs.

"The stratum of largest academic libraries, which in 1969 spent $2 on books for every dollar spent on serials, by 1976 spent $1.23 for every dollar spent on books."[6] An example of what this actually meant could be seen at the University of Illinois where in 1977 "the annualization of the encumbrances for serials had reached a point where 70% of the total funds received for library acquisitions had to be committed to handle serial obligations".[7]

In 1976, Herbert S. White discussed the economics of journal publication. Inflation affected the numbers of individual subscriptions to private, association and university journal presses. The ever reliable customers, the research and academic libraries, felt the crunch as prices continued to rise and presses began dual pricing procedures. White aptly described it as "spiralling economic disasters which accelerate by feeding on themselves".[8]

Although Downes suggested that the easiest and most likely solution for libraries was the creation of a National Periodicals Center,[9] this has never come to pass and seems to have been dropped from all agendas. Numerous plans, strategies and theories fill the void of a centralized solution. Most of these are based on title-by-title journal evaluation according to predetermined variables. The variables can be sorted into two main groups which Broude called negative and positive. An example of a negative variable is an element that detracts from value, such as excessive cost, and a positive value is one that enhances value, such as high impact factor.[10] Woodward alternately described the variables as of two orders, not giving either a pre-determined value. The first order is user-oriented and the second he calls availability.[11] With these variables identified, librarians can proceed to rank and discharge the least likely journals to be missed.

On consideration, however, it appears that this is not such an easy task. There is contention as to the qualifications of evaluators—are faculty or librarians or both together in varying degrees the most suited to do the job? According to Slote, H. Fussler contended that faculty should determine what goes or stays,[12] Slote refuted this.[13] Broude's study revealed that his faculty relied on but two variables—price and the professional affiliation of the journal—whereas librarians considered many more factors and, in an experimental study, from an exactly similar list of journals made wholly different deselection choices.[14]

There are those, wrote Fry, who contend that in the end, the process is wholly or largely a political one.[15] Acknowledging the tactical element in politics, Durey cautioned librarians to give faculty the feeling that they are being consulted every step of the way.[16] The problem with formulae, however—no matter who designs them—is that although the algorithms may be precise this is not necessarily true of the thinking behind them.[17]

As an alternative to all deselection, White suggested that the federal government intervene and recompense authors for page charges which would be made by journal presses. This would lower prices for all subscribers, even to the point of lessening the necessity of deselection.[18] His second suggestion was in an essay contributed to Sul H. Lee's anthology: academic and research libraries should cease being measured and ranked by collection size. Competition between them would then virtually disappear and deselection would proceed fairly and easily tailored to the needs of particular libraries.[19]

Whether tackled from bottom or top, management's role is crucial. What many administrators fail to see is the journal problem in context, rather than as an isolate. By virtue of being a problem within a system, every effort to subvert it touches on other issues and sets off ripple effects. The chief administrator, director or head of the library, must be aware of the right and cautious political maneuvers needed to carry off journal deselection. In this case, knowing the library clients and how they use the collection as well as the library professional staff and how they serve the users is essential. Osborne[20] and Subramanyam emphasized the importance of this in light of the fact that users' needs and foci frequently change, a process complicated by the fact that journals change as well.[21] Changes can only be tracked by a vigilant professional library staff and administration.

To this end, Segal created the CREW method—Continuous Review, Evaluation, and Weeding. His object was book deselection but his system[22] offers interesting possibilities for journals as well. The practice of constant review is one White claimed is done regularly in special libraries, the model of which academic libraries should follow. This is an echo of some library administrative literature that admonishes academic libraries to pick up business techniques, particularly that of forecasting obsolescence, with regard to the needs of the institution or organization. Successful companies seem to know when to drop an unsuccessful venture; White said that these same company (special) libraries do this as well and academic and research libraries should follow suit regarding the use of their journals.[23]

This, of course, brings us to a divisive issue—the value of the use study. If a journal in question is used, it is assumed it is needed—or isn't it? If it weren't there, would it be needed anyway or would some other item be used, justifying Mooer's law that use depends largely on ease of use? If the library stocks its shelves and apportions its money on the basis of present use, then what about its responsibilities to future scholarship? The argument of the *Scholarly Inquiry* was in favor of the use principle;[24] the response of several respondents to the report, particularly Gaulle, is against it. Gaulle contended that scholarship is served by the struggling private academic presses and should be supported by libraries regardless of statistical use counts.[25]

Nonetheless, there are vociferous advocates of use studies. Line's study led him to conclude that *only* use analyses should count; neither citations nor rankings by any other factor are important.[26] Thoughtful librarians might ask, if this be so, is there a concurrent responsibility to increasing use in the library? If a journal were to be discontinued because it is not used, perhaps libraries have to consider means and ways to increase use. Morse interestingly suggested reshelving by means of mathematical formulae based on common elements insuring exposure through proximity, rather than neighboring alphabetically by title within larger disciplines.[27]

Upon examination, the issue is not an easy one, and the more theoretical literature referred to above suggests a variety of questions that have no simple answers. Therefore, librarians seeking a deselection method might be interested in those publications dealing with specific models used and tested in academic institutions.

EVALUATION VARIABLES

The Variety

Numerous articles reviewed by this author discuss deselection projects of the past in which libraries chose particular variables with which to evaluate periodicals. Most describe how and why these choices were made. Some authors, e.g., Broude, worked with evaluation-type formulae where variables combine in weighted algorithms and were applied equally to all titles under consideration;[28] Others used various discretionary measures and the rule of exceptions, applying some but not all variables to an item. Unfortunately, there has been no standarized deselection procedure.

Interestingly, over the years, the number of variables in use increased. Thus, an article by Maxin in 1976 mentioned four;[29] Wenger and Childress, in 1977, mentioned six;[30] by 1978, Kraft and Polacsek employed fourteen.[31]

The variables could be described as Woodward does—each belonging to one of two sets: the user-oriented variables and the bibliographic ones.[32] The first group would contain in-house usage, circulation, interlibrary loan (ILL) data, inclusion of home faculty publications, appearance as a reference in doctoral theses of the home institution, use in curriculum, local research and by specific known user groups, length of run in the library, and duplication in the collection.

These differ from the many bibliographic variables which evaluate the journal by its citation frequency, physical size or bound volume shelf space, subscription price, processing costs, indexing and abstracting availability, regional or nearby ILL availability, presence in consortia or network commitments, language, national origin or starting publication date, appearance in major bibliographies, outcome of Bradford-Zipf application, impact factor, paper and printing quality, microform availability and self-contained indexing.

Yet a third grouping can be made of the non-quantifiable variables such as the discipline's place in future planning of the institution, the publisher's reputation, inclusion in the institution's accreditation requirements, and the relationship to the library's collection development policy.

At first glance, some of the many variables above may seem more important than others, a problem which has lent itself to weighting.

Amongst these, circulation data—which may be more familiar to librarians as it has been long a test for use/demand—often has been assigned a proportionately large weight, whereas other factors seen as the result of speculation, although no less important, e.g., the disciplines' place in future planning, have a lesser influence. Perhaps one reason why the number of variables has increased in recent years is the increased accent on accountability: the more the library has had to justify its operations, the more emphasis has been placed on service rather than size, accessibility rather than organization and preservation, and the more the library has been made to feel responsible to the reader. This burden forced librarians to ask just one more question and consider just one more factor before cancelling a subscription.

Back in 1971, and prior to the parameters of this study, Bernard Houghton could say with aplomb that application of the Bradford-Zipf bibliograph will tell you which journals make up the greatest proportion of titles in use. Very briefly, Bradford demonstrated that in a large collection of journal references, most of the articles on a particular subject came from a small number of titles. Based on that theory if, for example, 180 journals of 316 in a particular library account for 90% of journal use, Houghton claimed the library could eliminate most of the more than 100 titles in the 10% category of the non-used journals without disrupting the quality of service.[33] This might amount to an annual ruling by a particularly large group of readers and would be unacceptable as a deselection policy today. By 1982, Andrew Peters had listed usage as but *one* of three major factors, each made up of several elements and each receiving a weight to be entered into an algorithm, the algorithm itself being an expansion of the Kraft and Polacsek 1978 formula.[34]

The Most Often Employed Variable: USE

With all the discussion of appropriateness of the "use" variable and regardless of the increase in number of variables, use does remain the most often employed variable.

"No measure of journal use other than the one derived from a local-use study is of any significant practical value to libraries" wrote Maurice B. Line.[35] At this point in time, the simplistic nature of Line's statement seemed to ignore the difficulties in determining the proper time-frame for such a study. Regardless, few librarians would cancel a journal knowingly in heavy use independent of or relative to the rest of the collection. Wenger and Childress addressed the problem of time in their project at two NOAA libraries over a six month period by doing a sub-study after the first three months. The data from the three- and six-month studies led them to conclude that a three-month study would have been sufficient, the second three months' data not adding any significant information.[36] They cautioned though that use studies are inherently deficient and data should be employed "only as a filtering device".[37]

The thoroughness of their study points to yet another difficulty in use studies—the expense of monitoring. Wenger and Childress' hourly charting and use of signs and other types of written communications with users must have at least been time consuming, adding to work loads or prioritizing over other tasks, if not monetarily expensive. Consider the University of New Mexico's Medical Center Library's study[38] where special time-scoring sheets were designed and sent to all FTE faculty with the rank of assistant professor and above. Departmental ratings and overall faculty ratings were scored separately and then correlated. The author did not indicate how much this study cost. One can only speculate that much labor was involved.

Some studies were, by comparison, brief. At the University of Minnesota, use data was collected in two separate one-week periods[39] and University of South Carolina librarians devised a deselection system that allowed three librarians to complete the evaluation of 910 journals in four months, using the faculty as evaluators and applying variables to their choices afterwards.[40] Even if costs of use studies were statistically arrived at it would be hard to anticipate post-study cost. Librarians at University of California (Riverside) likened their two years of post-study paperwork to a divorce settlement![41]

The Least Used Variables

In contrast to wide attention to "use" as a variable, some librarians have identified factors used in only one or two journal deselection projects. One example is in Amir's science journal evaluation, which looked favorably upon those publications in which the work of his institution's faculty had been published.[47] A second example is in both the studies of Kraft & Polacsek[48] and Williamson,[49] where paper and printing quality were considered. This was an unusual but enlightened factor given the present concern and expense involved in library preservation projects. A third factor that was mentioned in but one source was that of the self-contained index.[50] This is a significantly useful tool for browsers despite its lack of thorough coverage of the field when compared with independent indices, such as *Science Citation Index*.

Only Bolgiano looked upon intensive journal monitoring as a collection evaluation tool in addition to a deselection process. If her estimation of the process of measuring of a journal's worth were to lead to cancellations, well and good, but, if not, the educational value of the procedure should not be underestimated.[51]

Mid-Spectrum Variables

Broude's journal formula $D = P + U + C + I + A + F + R$ displayed the mid-spectrum variables, where D = the total value; P = price; U = average annual use; C = impact factor; I = number of indexes and abstracting tools pointing to it; A = availability at area libraries for ILL; F = reputed rank of professsional organization publishing the journal; R = subjects' relatedness to curriculum.

Each variable appears to be quite a different element and at first glance it would seem that one has to add apples and oranges, a highly unlikely way to arrive at a total value. The solution arrived at was to assign a percentage to each factor, the whole to equal 100. Arrival at the percentages was attained through averaging the estimates of seventeen librarians involved in the project. For example, on Factor "P", two librarians might have decided its value, relative to the whole, was 20%; two others might have elected 15% or 5%. The various percentiles were added and averaged to arrive at a final one operable in all title evaluations for factor "P", in this case it was 13%.

The next step was to convert the dollar price to some integer between 1 and 13 for use in the formula. Here a conversion scale was elaborated so that the actual price could be reformulated. Since the higher the price—all things being equal—the less desirable the journal, the lower the price the more of the 13 points awarded the journal.

Formulae do require manipulations. Slote called them the products of imprecise thinking expressed in precision.[46] Most of the formulae in use in deselection appear to be the best expression to be expected given the situation.

The value of Broude's formula for some librarians may well be in the spelling out of the most important variables.

A CASE STUDY AND A DESELECTION MODEL

A literature survey such as this raises the following questions: hasn't enough work been done to elicit a journal deselection model that would be applicable to any academic or research library? Why have libraries repeated each others' mistakes or selected options and applied them without testing them? Why are even the carefully engineered projects later dismantled or disempowered as sudden monies or change of heart/power lead to reinstatement of many of the journals withdrawn?

In this section of the paper, I would like to follow one case at a University where I participated in the deselection process, Ben Gurion University of the Negev, Israel. In recalling the program design and procedures, and in light of the readings referred to above, analyses of mistakes and contributions can be made to facilitate a deselection model.

Israel's economic problems and rate of inflation make the United States' situation appear an imperturbable rock of stability. At great disadvantage to American universities, Israel must purchase most of its monographs and journals from abroad, or through dealers who do the same, in foreign currency.

Ben Gurion University of the Negev (BGU) is a young institution, some 12 years old. It has two main campuses in the city of Beersheva, Israel, called the "old" and the "new" campuses, each with libraries. A third campus is located some forty minutes out into the desert, at Sde Boker, and houses two important research institutes: the Desert Research Institute and the Ben Gurion Research Institute and Archives, each with its own library. BGU opened on the old campus with several departments of science, and although some of these remained there—among them biology and engineering (to be transferred eventually), some relocated to the new campus—among them physics and mathematics. The university's central library is on the new campus and houses the collections of the social sciences, the humanities, and some of the sciences. The medical school, with its own library, is also located on the new campus but, as it has its own management and funding, is excluded from this study. On its three campuses, BGU has over 6000 undergraduate and graduate students. The central library and branches own some 300,000 volumes and subscribe to about 4000 journals.

The BGU libraries are directed by a faculty member, a full professor, who holds a temporary and part-time position and a full-time assistant director, neither of whom are librarians. Organizationally, the library is divided into three major departments: serials; technical services, which includes acquisitions and cataloging; public services, which includes circulation and a small central reference department, separate staff for each of its three floors on which are housed the collections for the faculties of humanities, social sciences and sciences and three bibliographers—one for Judaica, one for the Fine Arts, Literature and Philosophy, and one for Science. Only the first two of these bibliographers, as well as the Education and Behavioral Sciences Departments liaison do monograph and journal selection.

In December of 1983 the library Director passed on to the library professional staff an order received from the University Rector to reduce the periodicals budget by 20% for the following academic year. The staff was asked to come up with a plan within one month to accomplish this task. The atmosphere was crisis-like as if a large corporation had asked its workers to reduce the electricity bill by 20% when each worker only knew about his/her own office and desk lamp.

As it turned out, this lack of total participation in the running of the library and knowledge of its various entities characterized the deselection procedure; it became segmented. At a subsequent meeting, various staff members made suggestions but no one plan was adopted by all. Each librarian was appointed one or more department(s) and subject area(s) to deselect and did so using some similar, some dissimilar, methods and criteria.

The librarian handling the humanities departments claimed that no suitable variables could be found to evaluate journals in his area. For example, he believed that impact factor was not an established measure for humanistic studies. He was going to refer each title back to its sponsoring department for judgment and evaluation.

In charge of Education and Behavioral Sciences with $5000 to cut, I saw that the task before us was not only important in terms of saving money but in terms of placing the library staff in a position to prove its competency and partnership in the educational enterprise of the university. I elaborated the variables I had chosen from the literature, and some I arrived at myself. Several staff persons, including the Sciences Librarian and Bibliographer, followed these. Others used them in part.

As certain as I was of the rightness of my choices when I began, both during and after the work difficult questions arose for me. As I discuss each variable, I will present these questions as well.

The material I was given to begin the work with was a computer print-out of each department's budgeted subscriptions, both inactive and active with some non-deciphered codes (including one I later learned meant that the subscription was shared by two departments). I crossed out the discontinued titles, translated the codes, taped ruled sheets of paper alongside the printed sheets and entered the most recent price which I verified from various bibliographic sources, such as Ulrich and Faxon.

The faculty members of the departments I worked with were fine people but only a small percentage took an active interest in the library. For each of these their interest was by and large in their chosen fields of research and teaching. I suspected that turning over the bibliographic data to the faculty for their judgment would result in a diluted unbalanced collection showing strength only in favored areas; I did not want that.

From the literature I felt I had gathered the most important journal worth factors to be measured: impact on research, physical accessibility, entry in major indexing tools, cost, and actual use. What I discovered in checking all these factors was that some of the information couldn't be found, some was out of date, some inaccurate, and some not currently quantifiable. It was to be a long search.

The Impact Factor (IF) was identified by Garfield at ISI and is listed yearly in the volume *Journal Citation Reports* that accompanies the series of citation indexes to the sciences, social sciences and humanities.[52] The IF is a measure of the number of times a journal is cited divided by the number of articles it prints, per year. There are two problems with the use of the IF as a measure of worth. One, not all the journals to be checked were listed. Two, in numerous areas and subdisciplines, monographic literature was equally if not more important than journal literature and is both the citer and the cited by the journal literature. This is not reflected in the IF.

Physical accessibility means that the item is actually present in the library and on its shelf or is readily available on interlibrary loan (ILL). Although a national union list for periodicals exists in Israel both in hard copy and COM format, it is not completely accurate nor up-to-date. ILL is itself problematic even assuming that the entries are reliable. A small university that does little lending itself is not high on the priority list of multiversities such as the Hebrew University in Jerusalem. Furthermore, if one other university claimed that title, what assurance had I that it would not be discontinued there in these stressful economic times?

Is cost a factor to be realistically considered? *The whole point of the project was to save money and it would seem then that cost should be the most important factor. But, the whole point of the university was to support learning and research.* Would the University consider hiring inadequate instructors at low salaries to save money? If a high-priced journal was highly valued and used was this not enough to ensure its maintenance? On the other hand, its price might well equal the price of three other journals—all other things being equal. If three could be kept by eliminating one, shouldn't that be the decision?

The inclusion of the journal in indexes presents another dilemma. Which indexes? Does this not entail another study on which indexes are used and how to increase use of indexes by bibliographic instruction? Indexing also involves another aspect—the extent of the library's holdings of the journal. Libraries are prone to favor those journals of which they have the most complete holdings, perhaps because of the prevalence of self-citations, or perhaps because of some other nonquantifiable "feeling" that it is hard to discontinue something collected so faithfully over a long period of time?

How is relevance to be measured? Relevant to whom or what? The closest measure I could find would be the university course listings. A paraprofessional went back over four years of university course catalogs and made a separate card for each course and listed the number of times it was taught. Four years seemed to be a measure that would allow for professors' sabbatical leaves, which in Israel often extend to two years. Upon examination of the numerous cards, it was hard to find a journal that was "irrelevant."

The closest prepared measure of relevance is probably one of the evaluative tools, e.g., Bill Katz's *Magazines for Libraries.* In it the journals considered essential, even primary or "Basic", as Katz called them,[53] to a college library are listed by subject. I decided to use this tool.

But in Israel, relevance has another dimension. About 80% of the journals were in English, 15% in Hebrew, and the rest in French, German, and several other languages. The student body can read and write in English, but their level of textual comprehension is generally far from the academic level of the journals under evaluation. It could safely be said that the journals in languages other than Hebrew were being purchased primarily for the faculty. This led to a joint decision amongst all in the project not to consider deselection of Hebrew language journals at this point and along these criteria.

After arriving at a list of variables I assigned points, the same number for each variable: 5 points for a complete journal run, 5 points if the journal price was average or below average price of all the journals in its discipline, 5 points if the journal attained an IF equal or above the average IF for all the journals in its discipline, 1-5 points for inclusion in the five most prominent indexes used in the discipline, 5 points if listed as a "Basic" journal in Katz's index, 5 points if the journal directly related to a course or courses taught for 3 of the 4 years checked. By the above calculations, a journal could rate thirty points maximally.

When I looked this over, I realized that absence of information, e.g., no IF, would skew the result considerably since it would be automatically assumed and rated as if the journal had a lower than average IF if none were listed. Therefore, in the absence of a measure for any factor, I considered the total points allowable only five times the number of measurable factors. Most journals would be able to earn maximally either 25 or 30 points. The number of points the journal accrued were then translated to a percentage of either 25 or 30.

Upon examination, one further adjustment had to be made and that for use. At BGU only bound English-language journals circulated and then only to faculty. There was no accurate measure of use to be obtained via circulation figures. There had been, however, an attempt to ascertain popularity of journals via a form stapled to unbound issues of journals as they arrived. This form asked a reader to sign his/her name, status as student or faculty and departmental affiliation. It was discovered that not all readers wanted to sign or bothered to and, if they did, they did not always give all the information requested. About the best use of this survey was to get a rough idea of the use of a journal. For that reason, I did not include it in my list of factors but adjusted the final score afterwards in accordance with this and other estimations of partiality by readers.

A year prior to beginning this project, I had compiled an index of all the journals pertaining to education and behavioral sciences with some bibliographical and content data appended. While doing this, I had surveyed the members of those respective departments as to their favored journals, and asked them to name what they considered "top priority" journals. In an attempt to utilize and balance these incomplete findings, I added five points to the resultant percentage score of the journal if it had been named a "top priority" and deducted five points from the percentage score if no unbound issue of the journal had ever been signed.

With scores for each of the almost 600 titles, I now had to define the cut-off point where eliminations would begin. These titles would then be sent first to the relevant department with an explanation procedure and finally to the rest of the faculties in order not to eliminate some vital journal that bypassed the examination by variables named above. When I had listed all the journals in order by score, it became clear that certain subjects would be totally eliminated having as a group acquired the lowest scores. In some cases, that might have been because the subject was a narrow one and only represented by one or two journals. I decided to prepare two lists of recommended cuts.

The first list would be that described above. The second required another examination of the journals and distribution by subject: e.g., separating education and behavioral sciences into such fields as cognition, communication, creativity, educational philosophy, religious education, and so forth. Each of these groups would contain a list of journals emphasizing their subjects and arranged by score. Elimination would proceed across the tables, one title per subject, that being the one with the lowest score, in its group, leaving at least one journal on each subject. In this second case, it occurred that some titles with higher scores were eliminated before others with lower scores. Both lists were presented to each department and the faculties were allowed to present opposition to the elimination of particular titles. As it turned out, they had few objections and were impressed and relieved that the library could perform this task for them as professionally as it did.

A deselection model cannot be replicated from this project. It was lacking in controls, lacking in substantiation, and largely empowered by intuition—as were most of the studies referred to in the literature review above!

Looking back I can see not only errors in the scientific construction of the project and enormous costs in staff time and energy, but administrative weaknesses. In any library looking for a journal deselection model, there appears to be two choices. One is to review the examples offered in the literature (each arising out of a unique situation in a unique library) and the other is to evaluate the capabilities of the library staff, their relationships to the faculty, and the unique features of the library itself.

For this reason, I would like to suggest not a journal deselection model per se but a simple administrative model to prepare for deselection and other contingencies.

Step 1. All professional librarians, whether in the Technical Services, Serials, or Reader Services division, whether subject specialists, bibliographers or departmental liaisons, should have an awareness of and an availability to the library budget and its allocations—i.e., how much each department or faculty is given to spend. This knowledge precludes a shocking exposé and prevents defensive reactions arising when the time comes to trim, share or otherwise reshape financial operations.

Step 2. A computer program should be designed to arrive at a numerical score for each journal based on bibliographic data such as those elements elaborated above. When a new journal is received, it, too, would be scored and also updated periodically as certain items, for example, price or index inclusion do change.

Step 3. The process of forecasting, adapted from the operations of successful business ventures, should be engaged in with regularity by the librarians. As new subjects flourish and develop, as faculty change and courses reform, librarians should be able to predict the need to balance their collections with regard to elimination or acquisition of new journals.

Step 4. The professional librarians should become familiar with the library clientele. This is what Downes called "intelligence based administration".[54] Active, aggressive communication will make the readers' habits and preferences a known factor in all decisions.

Without a philosophy of selection and deselection that calls for participatory management, and ongoing communicaiton between librarians and faculty, any library operation will smack of bureaucratic operatise that either shunts responsibility or looks for the quickest way to fulfill it without a view towards the future.

FOOTNOTES

1. Gellatly, Peter. Debits and a few credits: can serials prices be controlled? *Illinois Libraries.* 60:98-112; 1978 February: p. 101.

2. Presser, Carolynne. Collection management and serials in a changing library environment. *Serials Librarian.* 6(1): 59-67; 1981 Fall: p. 60.

3. Johnson, Steve. Serial deselection in university libraries: the next step. *Library Acquisitions.* 7:239-246; 1983: p. 240.

4. Bobinski, George. The golden age of librarianship. *Wilson Library Bulletin.* 58(5): 338-344; 1984 January.

5. Fry, Bernard M; White, Herbert S. Impact of economic pressures on American libraries and their decisions concerning scholarly and research journal acquisition and retention. *Library Acquisitions.* 3:153-237; 1979: p. 159.[Special Report]

6. *Ibid:* p. 171.

7. Huff, *Op cit:* p. 99.

8. White, Herbert S. Publishers, libraries and costs of journal subscriptions in times of funding retrenchment. *Library Quarterly.* 46(4);359-377; 1976 October: p. 376.

9. Downes, Robin N. Journal use studies in the management of journal collections in research libraries. In Lee, Sul, ed. *Serials collection development: choices and strategies.* Ann Arbor, MI: Pierian; 1981: p. 8.

10. Broude, Jeffrey. Journal deselection in an academic environment: a comparison of faculty and librarian choices. *Serials Librarian.* 3:147-166; 1978 Winter.

11. Woodward, A.M. *Factors affecting the renewal of periodical subscriptions: a study of decision-making in libraries with special reference to economics and inter-library loan.* London: Aslib; 1978; p. 51.

12. Slote, Stanley J., ed. *Weeding library collections—II.* 2nd rev. ed.: Libraries Unlimited; 1982: p.24.

13. *Ibid:* p.25.

14. Broude, *Op cit*: p.162.

15. Fry, *Op cit*: p.210.

16. Durey, Peter. Weeding serials subscriptions in a university library. *Collection Management.* 1(3-4): 91-94; 1976-77 Fall-Winter: p.94.

17. Slote, *Op cit*: p.52.

18. White, *Op cit*: p. 376.

19. White, Herbert S. Strategies and alternatives in dealing with the serials management budget. In Lee, Sul H., ed. *Serials collection development: choices and strategies.* Ann Arbor, MI: Pierian; 1981: p. 38.

20. Osborne, Charles B. Marketing the collection development aspects of serials control. In Lee, Sul H., ed. *Serials collection development: choices and strategies.* Ann Arbor, MI: Pierian; 1981: p. 16.

21. Subramanyam, K. Criteria for journal selection. *Special Libraries.* 66: 367-371; 1975 August: p. 371.

22. Segal, Joseph P. *Evaluating and weeding collections in small and medium-sized public libraries: the Crew method.* Chicago: American Library Association; 1980.

23. White, Herbert S. Publishers, libraries and costs. *Op cit:* p. 370.

24. National Enquiry into Scholarly Communication. *Scholarly communication: the report of the National Enquiry.* Baltimore: Johns Hopkins University Press; 1979.

25. Gaulle, Mary. Critiquing the National Enquiry by Bernard Goldman (and others). *Book Forum.* 5(1): 68-73; 1980: p. 71.

26. Line, Maurice B. Rank lists based on citations and library uses as indicators of journal usage in individual libraries. *Collection Management.* 2(4): 313-16; 1978 Winter: p. 313.

27. Morse, Philip M. Library models. *In*: Drake, A. W. et al., eds. *Analysis of public systems.* Cambridge: M.I.T.; 1972: p. 250.

28. Broude, *Op cit*: p. 150.

29. Maxin, Jacqueline A. Weeding journals with informal use statistics. *De-Acquisitions Librarian.* 1(2): 9-11; 1976 Summer.

30. Wenger, Charles B.; Childress, Judith. Journal evaluation in a large research library. *Journal of the American Association of Information Science.* 28:293-99; 1977 September.

31. Kraft, Donald H.; Polacsek, Richard A. A journal-worth measure for a journal selection decision model. *Collection Management* 2(2): 129-133; 1978 Summer: p. 130.

32. Woodward, *Op cit*: p. 3.

33. Houghton, Bernard. Zipf! *New Library World.* 73: 130; 1971, November.

34. Peters, Andrews. Evaluating periodicals. *College & Research Libraries.* 43: 149-50; 1982 March.

35. Line, *Op cit*: p. 313.

36. Wenger and Childress, *Op cit*: p. 293.

37. *Ibid*: p. 294.

38. Bess, Elvin D. Faculty participation in an evaluation review of use journals. *Bulletin of the Medical Library Association.* 66(4): 461-463; 1978 October.

39. Tibbets, Pamela. A method for estimating the in-house use of the periodical collection in the University of Minnesota Bio-Medical Library. *Bulletin of the Medical Library Association* 62(1): 37-48; 1974 January: p. 37.

40. Tomczyk, C. B. Journal and book deselection at USC Coastal Carolina. *South Carolina Librarian.* 26: 7-9+; 1982 Fall.

41. Wood, John B.; Coppel, Lynn M. [Seminar Moderators]. Periodicals deacquisitioning in academic libraries: proceedings of a seminar. Sponsored by the California Library Association. San Francisco, December, 1977. *Serials Librarian* 3: 315-331; 1979 Spring: p. 327.

42. Sprules, Marcia L. Online bibliometrics in an academic library: why the periodical selection studies done in special libraries are difficult to replicate in an academic setting. *Online.* 7:25; 1983, January.

43. Huff, *Op cit*: p. 101.

44. Slote, *Op cit*: pp. 98-133.

45. Broude, *Op cit*: p. 150-58.

46. Slote, *Op cit*: p. 52.

47. Amir, Michael J.; Newman, Wilda B. Information: unlimited demands-limited funds (testing the viability of a science journal collection in light of economic realities). *Collection Management.* 3(1): 111-119; 1979 Spring.

48. Kraft & Polacsek, *Op cit*: p. 130.

49. Williamson, Marilyn L. Serials evaluation at the Georgia Institute of Technology Library. *Serials Librarian.* 2(2): 181-192; 1977 Winter: p. 184.

50. Williamson, *Op cit*: p. 184.

51. Bolgiano, Christina E.; King, Mary Kathryn. Profiling a periodicals collection. *College & Research Libraries.* 39: 99-104; 1978 March: p. 99.

52. Institute for Scientific Information. *Journal Citation Reports.* Philadelphia: Institute for Scientific Information; 1973-.

53. Downes, *Op cit*: p. 17.

Journal Weeding in Relation to Declining Faculty Member Publishing

Tony Stankus

ABSTRACT. In light of financial and housing constraints a new exclusionary budgeting alliance for expensive, space-consuming specialty journals may be forced between academic sci-tech librarians and only those faculty whose publications activity and grantsmanship help support the library. In stringent circumstances the needs of productive scholars for new titles and shelf space must often be met by the business-like reassignment of the funds and space given over to scientists whose research publishing careers are over. Reliable, unobtrusive methods of determining when a scientist's apparent cessation of publications is likely to be permanent are discussed. The human circumstances surrounding an individual's termination of publishable research are discussed in conjunction with findings from the Sociology of Science. A highly professional, nonjudgmental style of informing the faculty member of intent to proceed and negotiating the cancellations is outlined.

INTRODUCTION

Science librarians may well feel caught between the demands of tenured faculty for continued subscriptions to their favorite specialized journals even as new faculty in different specialties are hired. The situation has become particularly acute in the case of costly and voluminous science journals in small libraries, particularly those at competitive liberal arts colleges. At these institutions, prestige-and-cost-conscious top administrators may feel that the abundance of job-seeking Ph.D.'s allows for increased publication and grants-winning expectations of their existing untenured faculty.

Tony Stankus is Science Librarian, Science Library, College of the Holy Cross, 1 College Street, Worcester, MA 01610. He took his BA, *Summa Cum Laude,* from that institution and his MLS from the University of Rhode Island at Kingston.

Those faculty that do not produce can be readily replaced. Yet librarians seeking to give these younger scientists a fighting chance may not be able to 'get either the initial funding or added shelf space from these same administrators. This paper suggests that there can be a rational way out of this dilemma based on a reexamination of those tenured faculty whose research careers appear to be over, with a reassignment of "their" funds and shelf space to more productive scholars. Two premises underly this approach:

— That in an increasing number of cases representation of a faculty member's specialty journals in the library collection can no longer be regarded as a perquisite of tenure or seniority. It must become a visible sign of an implicit understanding between the librarian and the individual faculty member. The librarian is doing his best to aid the faculty member in his research and the faculty member is doing his best to turn out the papers that bring in the grants dollars whose overhead deductions help support the library.
— That the advanced specialty journals targetted for cancellation are rarely intellectually accessible or of interest to faculty outside their specialties or to most students. Cancellation of this type of journal rarely involves "innocent victims" since most small colleges avoid closely duplicating subject specialists. Undergraduates moreover are rather closely directed in their advanced reading by their research advisors, faculty reasonably assumed to be active.

BACKGROUND

This study is part of an ongoing series on the career-long interactions of scientists and their journals and its meaning for subscription management. The first work[1] dealt with the surprising predictability of the specialty journal preferences of young scientists when librarians took into account the journals favored by their Ph.D. advisors and other journals frequently cited in those journals. A second study[2] dealt with highly prolific midcareer scientists and their propensity to invest some of their papers tentatively in brand new journals devoted to their specialties, with a majority of initial contributors eventually making the new journal a favorite outlet. This study deals with scientists, who for one reason or another, have disengaged from research and grantsmanship and whose journals are thereby ripe for cancellation. It contains both a search for reliable indicators of research death after which cancellations may be initiated, as well as a quest for an understanding of why these professors are neither continuing on the journal paths of their advisors nor venturing into new journals to call their own.

METHODS

Fifty-three recipients of Ph.D.'s in Chemistry employed at 34 small, competitive liberal arts colleges were identified through a scan of the directory *Research in Chemistry at Private Undergraduate Colleges.*[3] Faculty identified had indicated no publications for at least a five-year span. Their earlier publication histories were then traced via a tabulation of entries in the author indexes of *Chemical Abstracts.* A few younger, but equally inactive faculty had their histories traced by the more convenient "Source Index" of *Science Citation Index.* All of the identified professors had earned their degrees after 1961, a time frame chosen to generally eliminate consideration of soon-to-be-replaced elderly faculty members. To a surprising degree the group were graduates of America's better-rated graduate programs and were employed at highly selective institutions, schools which, while emphasizing undergraduate instruction, encouraged publications for tenure and promotion. Virtually all had access to rather creditable journal holdings, (a factor hearteningly and highly correlated to productivity[4]), many in separate science libraries on campus.

HOW CLOSELY RELATED IS AGE TO CESSATION OF PUBLICATION?

Professors in our study published their last papers at a wide variety of ages: from 24 to 57 (see Figure 1). Two findings are immediately apparent. While there seems to be a significant number of cessations at ages 27-30, there seems to be no clear-cut chronological age at which, as a general rule, chemistry professors who will eventually quit publishing, in fact, do quit. A cancellation policy based purely on age then would not only be discriminatory, it would not be based on the collected experiences of this study group nor on any carefully drawn research of which this author is aware. Indeed it would have been rather easy to have identified from the same directory an equal number of chemists at matching ages or

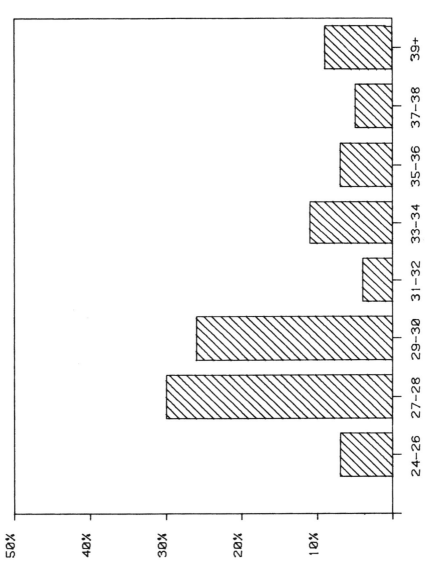

FIGURE 1. Age at last paper. While it is clear that many of our scientists cease publication between 27-30, there is no sure rule based on age alone that can guide cancellation policy.

older with continuously productive records. Nonetheless, some explanation of the rise in publication cessation at ages 27-30 is warranted. What seems to be happening to these chemists at such early stages of their careers?

ARRESTED CAREER DEVELOPMENT AND CESSATION OF PUBLICATION

Figure 2 shows the year after receipt of the Ph.D. within which those chemists who published had their last paper. Again, there are two significant findings. A large percentage of chemists seem to stop publishing within a few years of their Ph.D. A substantially smaller, but still noticeable group stops during their fifth and sixth post-Ph.D. year. A few interpretations are likely. One is that some newly minted Ph.D.'s quickly use up the publishable material developed during their dissertation, and, either through a poverty of ideas, time or materials, never seem able to publish again. Some support for this explanation lies in the fact that the median number of publications of authors in this group (203) approximates the independent findings of both Porter[5] and Stankus[6] concerning the numbers of papers typically derived from the dissertations of two separate groups of biochemists (3 and 2.67, respectively).

An explanation of the somewhat larger number of chemists ending their research output in post-Ph.D. years five and six might well center on a last effort to fulfill tenure requirements. By the end of year six, many of these chemists will have stood for tenure. Indeed, 86% of those who will have written their last paper had done so by then. This finding ties in with the somewhat larger numbers of chemists who stopped publishing between the ages of 27 and 30.

THE WAKE

Figure 3 is a display based on hindsight. It is an attempt to answer the question of how long must a librarian wait to be sure the faculty member's career is dead, not just sleeping. It shows the percent of eventually correct cancellations assuming a cutoff of subscriptions after given waiting periods. It uses the gap between the next-to-last and last papers as a test period.

When the spacings between all of the faculty member's papers are examined an interesting finding comes to light. When a faculty member exceeds his own longest previous gap without a paper, he is

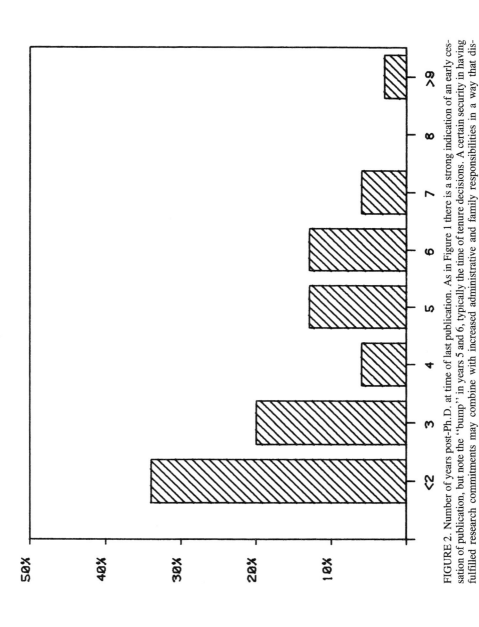

FIGURE 2. Number of years post-Ph.D. at time of last publication. As in Figure 1 there is a strong indication of an early cessation of publication, but note the "bump" in years 5 and 6, typically the time of tenure decisions. A certain security in having fulfilled research commitments may combine with increased administrative and family responsibilities in a way that discourages continued publications.

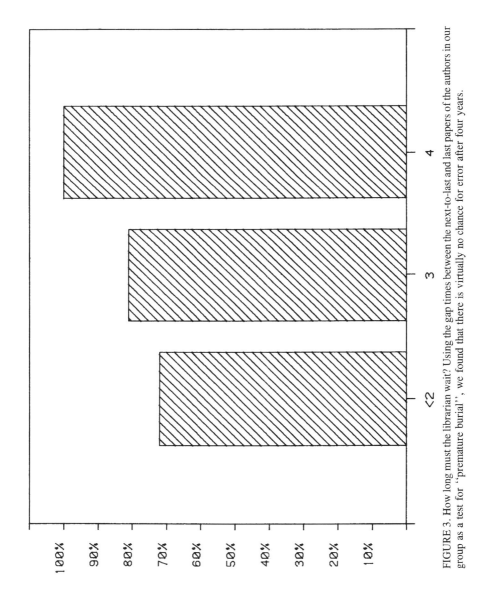

FIGURE 3. How long must the librarian wait? Using the gap times between the next-to-last and last papers of the authors in our group as a test for "premature burial", we found that there is virtually no chance for error after four years.

likely to have stopped altogether. It seems that a faculty member's publishing career rarely slows down and still continues successfully. Bensman has noted:[7] "Highly productive young scientists later maintained or increased their productivity, while young scientists who produced very little initially produced even less later . . . "

Two human circumstances provide a sympathetic explanation of how this situation can come about. The first deals with family responsibilities. The late twenties to mid-thirties represent the principal years of early childrearing for most college-educated couples. The second circumstance is the mixed blessing of being appointed to higher administrative duties. In smaller institutions where this "promotion" does not greatly increase access to funds, instrumentation, or support personnel, it is both an obligatory "honor" and a research distraction to be appointed or elected chairman, premedical advisor, faculty senator, or chronic committeeman. The role of both family and administrative pressures has been discussed by Sinderman:[8] "Sooner or later many runners elect to get off the fast track voluntarily . . . often scientists-turned-administrators find their scientific skills obsolete if too many years have intervened since publication of their last scientific papers."

NEGOTIATING THE CANCELLATION

The toughest part of cancellation management is telling the concerned faculty member. Not telling the faculty member is unprofessional via either arrogance or cowardice. Keys to successful cancellations include:

— Having the facts straight before negotiating.
— Adjusting the level of explicit spoken argumentation to the level of resistance.
— Avoiding giving the impression of passing judgment on the faculty member's overall value to the school.
— Avoiding letting the matter become personal.

The factual information of which the librarian should be sure prior to a meeting with the candidate includes:

— The actual record of the faculty member's publications, including not only papers and book chapters but printed convention abstracts and invited talks.

— The costs and space consumption of the existing publications and the proposed savings that will result. (The identity of any proposed beneficiary of reassigned funds or space need not be revealed initially.)
— The assurance that there is little reasonable likelihood of disciplinary crossover damage through the proposed cancellations.
— A backup plan of providing some coverage in the subject field through awareness services like *Current Contents,* broad overviews services like the *Annual Reviews* services and legitimate document delivery systems like *The Genuine Article* or Copyright-Clearance-Center-paid interlibrary loans.
— A backup plan of alerting the faculty member to library holdings in fields for which he may now hold some new responsibility: higher eduction administration, issues in premedical education, faculty evaluation, etc.
— Fallback lines of compromise in terms of given journals that must go even if others stay.

In the best of circumstances there is little need for extensive explanation. The faculty member views himself as quietly having made a change in emphasis in his career. He tells himself that he is now simply consenting to a discreet change in library holdings. A gratuitously elaborate explanation of the librarian's reasoning might be counterproductive.

In the worst of circumstances the faculty member questions the "nerve" of the librarian in making such an assessment. The proper response is a calm offer to let the College Dean or Treasurer arbitrate, including in the librarian's submission to those officers an estimate of the annual cost of subscriptions multiplied by the number of years the faculty member has until retirement, with adjustments for inflation and building costs. As a practical matter, few inactive faculty wish to have the top administration reminded just how inactive they are, or just how expensive the soothing of their indignation might be.

It is in the intermediate situation of a faculty member requesting continuance for advanced instructional support that the librarian must be prepared to give and take with a mix of confidence in generalized student collateral reading behavior that might be tempered by local exceptions. Stankus[9] has demonstrated that the most widely adopted Biochemistry texts rarely suggest readings in specialty research journals, overwhelmingly stressing instead more readable overview articles in *Science, Nature, Scientific American* and in hardbound continuing series such as the *Annual Reviews . . .* The professor might still insist that his assignments (and his own level of preparation) go beyond the textbook. A reasonable compromise is a mutually agreed upon test of the actual amount of use of contested titles (via reserve room housing) for three cycles of having the pertinent courses taught. If in these days of student evaluation, the professor successfully risks forcing the use of these difficult materials on his students, he has made his point. If an argument remains, in spite of student disuse, that the material is necessary for his own professional updating, and the professor is not receptive to a combination of current awareness services and legitimate document delivery, suggest that he take tax-deductible personal subscriptions.

SUMMARY

Rising costs and shrinking shelf space can force librarians to purchase and house specialty subscriptions for active scientists at the expense of the subscriptions and space allotted for their inactive colleagues. A study of the research careers of 53 liberal arts college chemists who eventually stopped publishing suggests that after a four-year interval without a paper, the librarian can reasonably infer no further papers are ever again likely to appear from that author, and can negotiate at least some specialty journal cancellations. The arguments against this policy are anticipated and a negotiating strategy is suggested.

REFERENCES

1. Stankus, Tony. Negotiating journal demands with young scientists using lists derived from thesis advisor records. *Collection Management.* 5 (3/4): 185-198, 1983 Fall/Winter.
2. Stankus, Tony. New specialized journals, mature scientists, and shifting loyalties. *Library Acquisitions Practice and Theory.* 9 (2), 1985 Spring, in press.
3. Andreen, Brian, editor. *Research in chemistry at private undergraduate colleges.* Minneapolis, MN: Council on Undergraduate Research; 1979.
4. Spencer, James N.; Yoder, Claude H. A survey of undergraduate research over the past decade. *Journal of Chemical Education.* 58 (10): 780-786, 1981 October.
5. Porter, Alan L. et al. The role of the dissertation in scientific careers. *American Scientist.* 70 (5): 475-481, 1982 Sept./Oct.
6. Stankus, Negotiating . . . p. 189.

7. Bensman, Stephen J. Journal subscriptions and acquisitions: The view from the library. A paper presented to the Annual Meeting of the Association of American University Presses. Spring Lake, NJ, June 18, 1984. (to appear in revised form in *College & Research Libraries*, 1985).

8. Sinderman, Carl J. *Winning the games scientists play.* New York: Plenum; 1982: p. 138.

9. Stankus, Tony. Collection development: journals for biochemists. *Special Collections.* 1(2): 51-74; 1981 Winter.

Original Language, Non-English Journals: Weeding Them and Holding Them

Virgil P. Diodato

ABSTRACT. There are several factors to be considered before discontinuing library holdings to non-English journals that are available also as translation journals. This paper demonstrates methods of collecting information about these factors. The author has discussed patron needs, subscription costs, citation patterns, and the availability of alternative translations. He has collected sample data about other factors: time lag and physical differences between the original and translation journals, coverage by indexing and abstracting services, and library holdings of the journals.

INTRODUCTION

How do sci-tech patrons and librarians in the United States deal with journal articles written in languages other than English? Some subscribe to translation journals. If a library is making available to its patrons both a translation journal and its original, non-English counterpart, under what conditions should the library weed out—discontinue—the subscription to the original language journal?

Definitions

For this article, an "original language journal (OLJ) is a journal that publishes non-English articles. A "translation journal" (TJ) is a journal that publishes only English translations of all or selected articles of a certain OLJ. For a given issue of a TJ, there usually is a corresponding issue of the OLJ. For example, *Biophysics* is a TJ

Virgil P. Diodato is Reference Librarian at Governors State University, University Park, IL 60466. He also teaches courses at the University of Wisconsin—Milwaukee School of Library and Information Science. He holds the PhD degree in Library and Information Science from the University of Illinois at Urbana-Champaign, IL.

that appears bimonthly, and its OLJ, *Biofizika,* also appears bimonthly. An OLJ-TJ "pair" is an OLJ and the particular TJ that is a translation of the given OLJ. So, *Biofizika* and *Biophysics* comprise an OLJ-TJ pair.

For convenience, a "subscription" to a journal includes any method of obtaining issues of the journal, whether that be by paid subscription, gift, exchange, or some other means.

The "test set" is a collection of eighty OLJ's and their corresponding eighty TJ's that I use as examples. See the Appendix for a list of the test set journals and for a description of how they were selected.

And, as implied in the Introduction above, I use a broad definition of "weeding" that includes the discontinuing of journal subscriptions.

Purpose

The purpose of this article is to identify factors to be considered if one is thinking about discontinuing an OLJ subscription. The article also will give examples of how to gather information about some of the factors.

Method

The process of writing this article probably has been somewhat analogous to the process that a new librarian or information specialist would go through upon being placed in charge of a collection that includes subscriptions to OLJ's and their TJ counterparts. Just as I was asked to write an article about OLJ's, the new librarian might be asked to think about discontinuing some OLJ subscriptions. For either of us a first step is to gather information, and so the rest of the article is a discussion of points I have encountered while trying to gather information about OLJ's and TJ's.

THE LITERATURE

For background reading about OLJ's and TJ's one can use both the journal literature and guides to the literature. The journal literature includes the *Science & Technology Libraries* Winter, 1982 issue, which was devoted to translations. One of the articles,

Fedunok, is a good review of problems associated with translations of scientific literature. Fedunok discusses OLJ's, TJ's, and other translation tools. She notes that "few library users are aware of those sources that do exist to track down translations . . . .In mastering this tricky and elusive literature the science and technology librarian is indeed providing an invaluable service . . . "[1] In other journal literature, Reynolds and Subramanyam provide a list of translated Russian chemistry journals. They feel that publishing cover-to-cover TJ's is a "more effective solution" to removing language barriers than is training scientists to read a new language.[2] Garfield finds that cover-to-cover TJ's have slowed the acceptance of English as a worldwide language of science because for Russian scientists "the knowledge that their leading journals will be translated into English relieves them of any compunction to write and publish in English, a requirement that scientists in other continents (that have little or no TJ service) have accepted."[3]

Sci-tech literature guides like Subramanyam[4] introduce readers to OLJ's and TJ's and describe other methods of obtaining translations, such as using the National Translations Center, the International Translations Centre, and the Joint Publications Research Service. Literature guides also point readers to reference works that list OLJ's and TJ's. These lists include Himmelsbach and Boyd[5] and *Journals in translation.*[6]

DECISION MAKING FACTORS

Deciding whether or not to discontinue on OLJ subscription can involve factors such as patron needs, subscription costs, OLJ-TJ time lag, citation patterns, coverage by indexing and abstracting services, physical differences between an OLJ and its TJ counterpart, availability of alternative translations, and the OLJ-TJ holdings of other libraries.

PATRON NEEDS. The need of the patron is the most important factor to weigh against all the others discussed here. How vital an OLJ is to patrons means asking questions like: Does the OLJ become available long before its TJ does? In what ways is the content of an OLJ issue different from that of its TJ counterpart? Do patrons have different uses for the OLJ and TJ, perhaps taking time-valued information from the OLJ and information of peripheral interest from TJ's? Typical user surveys might not answer these questions adequately, for the use of OLJ's could be so specialized that only direct probing of individual patron's needs and uses could divine the value of the OLJ. Librarians need to probe themselves, too, for in some situations the librarian is the prime patron of the collection. This is especially true when patrons require answers to their queries rather than directions as to how to obtain those answers.

An example of the need for probing involves the language barrier between patrons and the OLJ. Observation of patrons might determine that they have a use for an OLJ even though they do not speak and do not have good general reading skills in the OLJ language. So, the English-reading subject specialist could have very specific, limited, and yet very useful language abilities that allow him or her to ferret out information from articles written in that specialty.

SUBSCRIPTION COSTS. To subscribe to an OLJ and to its TJ counterpart means paying two fees for two versions of the same information. There are two payments regardless of whether gifts or exchanges are involved, for processing any material costs time and money. And it is easy to believe that a subscription payment for either the OLJ or TJ can cost more than for the typical sci-tech journal. The OLJ subscription is expensive because it is published in one country and must be shipped to readers in another country. The TJ is expensive because one must pay for the repackaging of information into another language. Garfield tells us that "[t]he existence of two versions of the same journal only adds to the bibliographic information overload that exists in the world today";[7] a library must pay for this overload. As with all the factors below, one must weigh subscription cost against the needs of patrons. Patrons might well need both versions of a journal or what Garfield calls "redundancy in scientific communication."[8]

OLJ-TJ TIME LAG. Repackaging OLJ articles takes time, and so a TJ issue will be published six to twelve months and sometimes even two years after the corresponding OLJ issue.[9,10] If the information in an article is more likely to be used for retrospective searching than for current awareness by certain patrons, then those people could be satisfied solely by the TJ version of the article. If the currency of information is important, however, the availability of the OLJ is vital.

Although an OLJ issue appears sometime before its TJ counterpart, one should ask if indexing and abstracting services always cover the OLJ issue before they cover the TJ issue. If, say,

Mathematical Reviews (MR) picks up both an OLJ article and its TJ translation in the September 1985 *MR* issue, this in some way could ameliorate the TJ time lag problem. If *MR* is our only access to this particular journal, then we will learn about both versions of the article at the same time. And it is possible that by the time *MR* reviews the article, both versions of the journal issue could be on the shelf.

I used the test set of OLJ-TJ pairs to study how TJ's and OLJ's compare in promptness of coverage by indexing and abstracting services. Online database searching is a convenient way to obtain this data, and I considered only those eighteen OLJ-TJ pairs covered by indexing or abstracting services searchable via DIALOG Information Services. (*Ulrich's international periodicals directory*[11] indicated which services covered which journals. See the COVERAGE section below.) As an example of data obtained via this method, consider the OLJ *Genetika* and its TJ counterpart, *Soviet Genetics*. In April, 1985, I searched the BIOSIS database by the names of both these journals. The first three *Genetika* articles given in BIOSIS were from the tenth of twelve monthly OLJ issues published in 1984, and the first three *Soviet Genetics* articles were from the third TJ issue of 1984. According to this method and assuming that the first articles listed by a database are the latest articles indexed (an assumption that need not be always valid), the time lag between the OLJ and the TJ is seven months. The method is crude, but in this case it does confirm that access via BIOSIS to this TJ is not as up to date as access to the OLJ. When using this method, it is important to be aware of whether, as in the examples given here, the OLJ and TJ use the same volume numbering system.

As expected, rarely—in two of eighteen cases—is indexing for a TJ issue available before indexing is available for the corresponding OLJ issue. For example, issue 1, 1984, of *Applied Solar Energy* has been picked up by the COMPENDEX database at the same time that the most recently indexed issue of the OLJ, *Gelioteckhnika,* issue 3, 1983, is in both COMPENDEX and INSPEC. The typical situation I have found, however—in fourteen of eighteen cases—is that the most recently indexed issue of a given OLJ is the same number and year as the most recently indexed TJ. Much of this is due to the INSPEC database including bibliographic data for both versions of an article in the same record.

CITATION PATTERNS. If authors, especially those authors who have access to both an OLJ and its TJ, cite articles appearing in the OLJ, this is some indication that the OLJ is useful. If your library's patrons have information needs that are similar to the needs of authors who cite an OLJ, you could reason that the OLJ therefore is useful to your patrons. It is not known if authors with equal access to OLJ's and TJ's tend to cite the OLJ more or the TJ more. For the librarian or information specialist, it might be helpful to ask patron-authors who do happen to have such a choice how they make that choice. Their responses could help us understand some of the differences between OLJ's and TJ's.

For the bibliometrician, it would be useful to identify authors who have access to both versions of a journal and yet cite only from the OLJ or only from the TJ. A rather tedious but workable method for a bibliometric analysis of citation preference would be to employ *Science Citation Index* or its online version, SCISEARCH, to identify authors who cite articles published in given issues of an OLJ or a TJ. Then a tool like *Chemical Abstracts service source index* would tell the bibliometrician if the author's local collection holds both the OLJ and TJ. Although all this information might indicate to the bibliometrician if authors with a choice tend to prefer the OLJ or the TJ, only direct communication with authors would suggest why they make their choices. Garfield has performed related studies by examining how often original language Russian journals receive any kind of citations. He finds that "most Soviet journals rank generally quite low . . . despite timely processing by . . . abstracting/indexing services."[12]

COVERAGE BY INDEXING AND ABSTRACTING SERVICES. Regardless of time lag and citation patterns, if few indexing and abstracting services used by a library's patrons cover a certain OLJ, then that OLJ becomes rather inaccessible, especially as part of the retrospective sci-tech literature. I used *Ulrich's international periodicals directory* to find out which services do cover journals in the test set. *Ulrich's* has indexing information for forty-one of the eighty test pairs. The results show that most—twenty-nine of forty-one—pairs have indexing coverage for both the OLJ and the TJ. A mean 3.0 indexing and abstracting services cover each TJ, while a mean 2.5 services cover each OLJ. Also, three of forty-one TJ's receive no indexing/abstracting coverage, according to *Ulrich's,* while nine OLJ's receive no coverage. English language biases of *Ulrich's* could account for much of the edge in coverage of TJ's. For twenty-four of the OLJ-TJ pairs, the OLJ is indexed by the same service that indexes the TJ. In most cases the service is *Chemical Abstracts;* this is not surprising, given that I used *Chemical*

Abstracts source index (CASSI)[13] as a means of selecting the test set journals. If you feel that *Ulrich's* indexing information is incomplete, you might prefer to get coverage data from sources such as jobbers' catalogs, OCLC union lists, and the pages of the journals and indexing/abstracting tools themselves.

PHYSICAL DIFFERENCES BETWEEN OLJ'S AND TJ'S. An OLJ issue can be quite different from its TJ counterpart, and such differences affect the relative value of OLJ and TJ to patrons. For example, an OLJ in mathematics might differ from its TJ in that the TJ fails to translate news notes; this could be a minor inconvenience to a physics library's patrons who find items in this mathematics journal to be of peripheral interest. On the other hand, a TJ in meteorology might have illustrations that are slightly fuzzy reproductions of those in the OLJ, a handicap for those readers who consider this TJ to be their prime source about meteorological research outside the United States.

A. Physical Differences Found in a Case Study. If backfiles of both an OLJ and its TJ are on hand, one can do a physical comparison of the two and thereby see how they differ. I performed such a page by page comparison with the 1981 issues of the mathematics section of *Vestnik Moskovskogo Universita, Seriya 1, Matematika, Mekhanika* and the 1981 issues of its TJ, the *Moscow University Mathematics Bulletin.*

The OLJ and TJ demonstrate minor differences in size and format, and in placement and translation of summaries. The TJ format seems more pleasing to the American reader. For example, the OLJ issues I examined stand about twenty-three centimeters high, while the TJ's are about twenty-six centimeters high, a situation not unusual for journals provided by the Allerton Press translation series. In the less cramped TJ format, each new article begins on a new page. In the OLJ, an article often begins on the same page where the previous article ends. The typical OLJ article has an English summary at its end, whereas this summary appears at the beginning of the TJ's article. Although the summary in each case is in English, the TJ apparently provides a translation of the Russian version of the summary rather than copying the OLJ's English summary. Keeping in mind that the English summary in the OLJ is probably also a translation of the original author's Russian summary, it is not surprising that the English summaries in OLJ and TJ show some very minor differences in expression.

The OLJ and TJ used in the case study uncover important facts about type quality of formulas and the selectivity of items to be translated. Rather than set type for all the many mathematical expressions, the TJ publisher has photoduplicated formulas that are not physically part of the narrative of an article. Thus, if a formula is centered between two paragraphs of text in the OLJ, so is it in the TJ. But the TJ formula is merely a reproduction of the formula that had been printed on the OLJ page. The OLJ issues I examined employed a type font that had very poor quality plus signs. The poor quality is duplicated in the TJ, for the TJ plus signs have blots and cracks identical to those in the OLJ. Although this can be an annoyance, photoduplication does insure that the formulas are translated without typographical errors. Even though users might call this TJ a cover-to-cover translation of the OLJ, there are some items that do not get translated. For example, a report on a meeting, a biographical note, and two pages of briefly annotated reviews appear in the OLJ but not in the TJ.

B. Physical Differences Found in the Test Set. As noted in the case study above, selectivity of translation can cause differences between an OLJ and a TJ. An analysis of the eighty OLJ-TJ pairs in the test set indicates that some OLJ's differ from their TJ's because the TJ's omit not merely news notes and biographical sketches but also some major articles. These TJ's are called "selected" translations, and *CASSI* labels three of the eighty test TJ's as selected translations. TJ's can be selective in another way, for a TJ might begin publication in 1967, while the OLJ began in 1950. Thus, seventeen years are without translation coverage—unless some other TJ had covered those seventeen earlier years. Of the eighty OLJ-TJ pairs in the test set, thirty-two have at least five years without translation coverage by their respective TJ's.

ALTERNATIVE TRANSLATIONS. A library might be holding on to an OLJ subscription because the TJ counterpart that the library receives has a poor reputation among patrons, perhaps because of physical differences, subscription costs, or any of the other factors mentioned above. The value of the OLJ could decrease if one compared it to another translation. Perhaps a second TJ, published and translated by sources different from those who work on the first TJ would satisfy the patrons to the point of making the OLJ expendable. However, there are a very few OLJ's that have more than one TJ simultaneously available. *Technical Cybernetics* and *Engineering Cybernetics* are TJ's, each translating *Izvestiya Akademii Nauk*

SSSR, Tekhnicheskaya Kibernetika articles from 1963 to the present.[14]

HOLDINGS OF OTHER LIBRARIES. Knowing whether or not other libraries hold a given OLJ can help your weeding decision about the OLJ in at least two ways. First, such awareness permits the creation of cooperative acquisition programs. If an OLJ held in one collection becomes accessible to patrons of another collection, then both collections might not need to hold the OLJ, as long as the cost of cooperation is not too high. Part of the cost of cooperation can be an unacceptably low level of access to some journals by some patrons. Second, awareness of the holdings of another collection, especially one similar to yours, helps because you can observe how your colleagues have handled weeding decisions similar to yours.

I have done an analysis of library holdings of the eighty OLJ-TJ pairs in the test set. The analysis consists of answers to four questions. Whatever the answers to those questions, you might find that asking a colleague, "What have you done . . . " about an OLJ provides as much useful information as does this analysis. Keep in mind that the analysis reflects the characteristics of the particular eighty journal pairs examined and that the holdings information gotten from *CASSI* reflects the characteristics of the tool, which provides United States holdings data for only 300 libraries, all of which have major research collections. One could examine a broader range of libraries by using a holdings tool like OCLC's union lists. The results below are for "current" holdings of OLJ's and TJ's, that is, holdings that include issues dated 1979, the latest year examined by the *CASSI* volumes used for the analysis. (See the Appendix for a list of holdings data.)

Holdings Question One. Does the typical research library have current holdings of many OLJ's? No, according to this analysis, for only thirteen of the 300 research libraries hold at least forty of the eighty test OLJ's. Most the of the libraries—196—have no more than nine of eighty OLJ's.

Holdings Question Two. Does the typical research library have many current holdings of OLJ-TJ pairs? No. Most research libraries—157 of 300—report no current OLJ-TJ pairs. However, there are seventeen libraries that have at least twenty such pairs. An interesting fact is that some libraries holding many OLJ's have very few TJ's. For example, one special sci-tech library holds forty-five OLJ's but none of their corresponding TJ's, and there is a university library that has fifty OLJ's but only seven of the corresponding TJ's.

Holdings Question Three. Is the above result confirmed if we consider only libraries that hold at least one current OLJ? Limiting the question to such libraries is important so that we can eliminate libraries that do not collect the OLJ's in the test set. There are 179 libraries with at least one current OLJ, and the results show that there is a tendency for these libraries to hold OLJ-TJ pairs rather than only the OLJ. On average (mean), the 179 libraries hold the TJ's for fifty-one percent of their OLJ's. Typical is one academic departmental sci-tech library that holds eleven OLJ's and six of the corresponding TJ's.

Holdings Question Four. Fedunok suggests that the number of subscriptions to TJ's might be decreasing over the years, due at least to the expense of subscriptions.[15] Is this true, for TJ's and for OLJ's? An indirect way to answer this is to compare libraries that hold current issues of a journal with libraries that hold *any* issue of that journal. For example, fifty libraries have on their shelves at least some issues of the OLJ, *Ukrainskii Khimicheskii Zhurnal,* but ten of these libraries report no current issues of that journal. So, one could infer that there has been at most a twenty percent loss of subscriptions to this journal. Using this method, it is possible to compare the rate at which OLJ's and TJ's have been discontinued by libraries. Only fourteen of the eighty OLJ's have had their holdings discontinued by twenty or more percent of the surveyed libraries. Libraries holding TJ's are even more loyal subscribers, for only seven TJ's have discontinued backfiles in twenty percent or more of their holding libraries. Thus, there is evidence that libraries are more likely to discontinue OLJ's than TJ's.

FINAL COMMENT

It is feasible to collect information for decision making about original language journals. A caveat to readers is that it is more important to consider the general methods of collecting information described here than to apply to their situations the data I happened to have collected. Thus, one might find that *Ulrich's* and *CASSI* are not the best tools with which to gather information about indexing coverage and library holdings. Nevertheless, where a journal is indexed and what libraries hold it are important facts that can help one decide whether or not to continue receiving the journal.

REFERENCES

1. Fedunok, Suzanne. Printed and online sources for technical translations. *Science & Technology Libraries.* 3(2): 10; 1982 Winter.
2. Reynolds, Stephanie A.; Subramanyam, K. An entry to foreign literature. *Chemtech.* 13(10): 582; 1983 October.
3. Garfield, Eugene. *Essays of an information scientist.* Philadelphia: ISI Press; 1977: vol. 1, p. 334.
4. Subramanyam, Krishna. *Scientific and technical information resources.* New York: Marcel Dekker; 1981: Chapter 17.
5. Himmelsbach, Carl J.; Boyd, Grace E. *A guide to scientific and technical journals in translation.* New York: Special Libraries Association; 1972.
6. *Journals in translation.* Delft: International Translations Centre; 1982.
7. Garfield, p. 104.
8. Garfield, p. 104.
9. Fedunok, p. 6.
10. Reynolds and Subramanyam, p. 582.
11. *Ulrich's international periodicals directory.* New York: Bowker; 1984.
12. Garfield, p. 335.
13. *Chemical Abstracts source index. 1907-1979 cumulative.* Columbus, OH: American Chemical Society; 1980.
14. Himmelsbach, Carl J; Boyd, Grace E. *A guide to scientific and technical journals in translation.* New York: Special Libraries Association; 1968: pp. 11-12.
15. Fedunok, p. 6.
16. *Guide to Soviet scientific-technical research journals in cover-to-cover translation.* New York: Allerton Press; 1984.
17. Himmelsbach; Boyd, 1968, pp. 1-13.

APPENDIX

A test set of eighty OLJ's and their eighty TJ counterparts provide data for various examples and analyses appearing in this article. Selection of the eighty was very subjective. I culled two tools, an Allerton Press catalog[16] and the 1968 edition of Himmelsbach and Boyd[17] for TJ's and OLJ's. Only those items having entries in *Chemical Abstracts service source index (CASSI)* appear here; further stipulations are that the *CASSI* record indicate that both TJ and OLJ in a given pair are not discontinued and that the TJ be labeled an "English Translation."

There follows a list of the eighty OLJ's, all of which have Russian as the OLJ language.

APPENDIX

OLJ CASSI Abbreviated Title	No. of CASSI Libraries Holding Current Issues of			Overlap[a] (%)
	OLJ	TJ	Both	
Akust Zh	24	125	18	14
Astrofizika	20	72	12	15
Astron Vestn	10	45	7	15
Astron Zh	41	110	32	27
At Energ	40	71	24	28
Avtom Svarka	10	18	7	33
Avtom Vychisl Tekh	11	44	4	8
Avtometriya	7	24	3	11
Biofizika	33	94	21	20
Biokhimiya	58	134	38	25
Byull Eksp Biol Med	22	98	18	18
Defektoskopiya	14	29	8	23
Dokl Akad Nauk SSSR [Biochem]	100	91	48	34
Dokl Akad Nauk SSSR [Biol Sci]	100	110	62	42
Dokl Akad Nauk SSSR [Biophys]	100	62	39	32
Dokl Akad Nauk SSSR [Bot Sci]	100	74	43	33
Dokl Akad Nauk SSSR [Chem]	100	109	58	38
Dokl Akad Nauk SSSR [Chem Technol]	100	68	45	37
Dokl Akad Nauk SSSR [Earth Sci]	100	96	63	47
Dokl Akad Nauk SSSR [Math]	100	135	72	44
Dokl Akad Nauk SSSR [Phys]	100	150	77	45
Dokl Akad Nauk SSSR [Phys Chem]	100	92	57	42
Elektrichestvo	39	59	26	36
Elektrokhimiya	19	69	13	17
Elektron Obrab Mater	13	19	8	33
Elektrosvyaz	20	99	17	17
Elektrotekhnika	13	34	4	9
Entomol Obozr	21	70	16	21
Farmakol Toksikol	29	19	7	17
Fiz Goreniya Vzryva	13	54	8	14
Fiz Khim Mekh Mater	11	61	3	4
Fiz Met Metalloved	28	100	20	19
Fiz Tekh Poluprovodn	8	62	5	8
Fiz Tekh Prob Razrab Polezn Iskop	8	41	3	7
Fiz Tverd Tela	30	147	24	16
Fiziol Rast	14	78	8	10
Geliotekhnika	10	57	4	6
Genetika	41	58	18	22
Geol Geofiz	32	31	13	26
Geol Nefti Gaza	15	71	9	12
Geomagn Aeron	16	61	8	12
Geotektonika	19	72	13	17
Gidrotekh Stroit	19	60	12	18
Gig Tr Prof Zabol	9	1	1	11
Inzh Fiz Zh	46	73	34	40
Izmer Tekh	20	88	13	14
Izv Akad Nauk SSSR Energ Transp	29	22	7	16
Izv Akad Nauk SSSR Fiz Atmos Okeana	37	67	22	27
Izv Akad Nauk SSSR Fiz Zemli	31	66	19	24
Izv Akad Nauk SSSR Mekh Tverd Tela	23	40	8	15
Izv Akad Nauk SSSR Mekh Zhidk Gaza	30	44	9	14
Izv Akad Nauk SSSR Met	29	41	12	21
Izv Akad Nauk SSSR Neorg Mater	16	51	7	12
Izv Akad Nauk SSSR Ser Fiz	51	80	35	36
Izv Akad Nauk SSSR Ser Khim	41	119	28	21
Izv Akad Nauk SSSR Tekh Kibern	29	84	22	24
Izv Vyssh Uchebn Zaved Aviats Tekh	18	24	3	8
Izv Vyssh Uchebn Zaved Fiz	17	58	8	12

APPENDIX, continued

OLJ CASSI Abbreviated Title	No. of CASSI Libraries Holding Current Issues of			Overlap (%)[a]
	OLJ	TJ	Both	
Izv Vyssh Uchebn Zaved Geod Aerofotos'emka	15	64	10	14
Iaz Vyssh Uchebn Zaved Radioelektron	14	43	5	10
Izv Vyssh Uchebn Zaved Radiofiz	16	49	3	5
Izv Vyssh Uchebn Zaved Tsvetn Metall	19	6	3	14
Khim Tverd Topl	13	27	5	14
Koks Khim	10	26	6	20
Kosm Issled	20	58	10	15
Kratk Soobshch Fiz	3	24	0	0
Liet Fiz Rinkinys	13	22	3	9
Meteorol Gidrol	25	32	7	14
Nauchno Tekh Inf Ser 1	6	17	3	15
Nauchno Tekh Inf Ser 2	4	18	1	5
Tsitol Genet	21	28	9	23
Ukr Khim Zh	40	54	17	22
Vestn Mosk Univ Ser 1 Mat	57	44	24	31
Vestn Mosk Univ Ser 1 Mekh	57	24	9	13
Vestn Mosk Univ Ser 2 Khim	35	38	12	20
Vestn Mosk Univ Ser 3 Fiz Astron	42	29	7	11
Vestn Mosk Univ Ser 4 Geol	27	22	8	20
Vestn Mosk Univ Ser 16 Biol	10	18	2	8
Vestn Mosk Univ Ser 17 Pochvoved	10	18	1	4
Zh Vses Khim O-va	17	20	0	0

[a] Overlap is the ratio of the number of libraries holding both an OLJ and its TJ to the number of libraries holding at least one of these versions. For the first journal, Akust Zh, the overlap is (18/(24+125-18)) x 100 = 14.

Records Management in an Architectural Firm: Skidmore, Owings & Merrill

Catherine R. Burke

ABSTRACT. The following paper describes the management of records at Skidmore, Owings & Merrill, a large architectural firm. Types of materials are discussed, along with organization, housing, control and retrieval. Special emphasis is placed on the practices and problems of weeding such a specialized collection.

INTRODUCTION

Skidmore, Owings & Merrill (SOM), founded in 1936, strives to provide complete professional services in the areas of architectural design, planning and engineering. The firm, with its family of nine major offices, has completed a variety of projects in the United States and over forty countries worldwide. While closely interacting with each other, the individual offices maintain a certain autonomy by assuming the responsibility of their own projects from start to finish. Some of the New York Office's contributions to the field have included Lever House, the various Chase Manhattan Bank Buildings, New Jeddah International Airport and the Kuwait Embassy.

The organizational structure at SOM is characterized by the team approach. A team nucleus is formed with an administrative partner, a design partner, a project manager, senior designers and technical personnel. This team completes one project from start to finish, maintaining the integrity of that project. A new team is then created for each ensuing project.

This team concept permeates every level of the New York

Catherine R. Burke holds an MLS degree from the University of Pittsburgh and is currently File Supervisor, Skidmore, Owings & Merrill, 220 East 42d Street, New York, NY, 10017.

© 1986 by The Haworth Press, Inc. All rights reserved.

Office's organizational structure, culminating in its design of a Central File Department. While the File Supervisor functions as head of the department and coordinates the activities of the Archivist and File Clerk, all three positions interact with the same team spirit for accomplishing a variety of tasks. The File Clerk organizes and files current correspondence and contracts related to jobs which are open to labor. The Archivist prepares older materials and drawings of closed jobs for warehouse storage and microfilming. The Archivist also serves as a liaison between the office and the storage facility.

A separate SOM corporate library is a resource center which meets the information requirements of all departments and employees. Besides providing ready reference, research and computer searching, the Librarian also serves as the Head of Information Services and supervises the Central File Department in an advisory capacity.

THE COLLECTION

Since SOM New York's inception, all active records have been housed in one centralized location. Massive amounts of correspondence and other materials must be at the ready disposal of project team members, and a centralized filing department has worked well for the firm.

Organization of Materials

The types of records kept by Central File consist of the following main categories:

— print
— graphics
— accounting
— models.

The system of organization of these materials has evolved over a period of time and recently has been standardized by the department.

Printed items make up a large part of SOM's records. As many as two hundred different projects are open to labor at one time. Each project has vital incoming and outgoing correspondence related to the job progress, cost estimates, building codes, construction, as well as the various technical reports, meeting minutes and specifications.

Graphics also constitute the bulk of any architectural firm's materials. Since a finished building is each team's goal, the architectural drawings related to that building are, in a simplified sense, the firm's "product". The various types of graphics held by Central File include: tracings, design sketches, preliminary drawings, shop drawings, presentations, architectural drawings, as well as the various sub-groups of electrical, plumbing, HVAC, zoning, building department, etc.

The Accounting Department also functions as a vital part of SOM's team. Besides issuing the various job numbers to each team project for identification and billing purposes, this department maintains a large file of contracts and other legal documents. They also produce various accounting reports and organize a great deal of other financial data. Once completed, these records then are turned over to Central File for filing.

Models of projects often are commissioned by clients in advance of construction. Sometimes, depending upon the complexity of the building, as many as five or six small scale versions are created in SOM's fully equipped Model Shop. While some models are returned to the client at the job's completion, others are used for display or future study. These are given over to Central File for storage.

Other miscellaneous types of materials include product samples, promotional materials, personal reading files, etc. These items, however, should be discarded before the completion of a project and do not comprise an important part of the Central File records.

Housing/Storage

Decisions for housing or storage are based upon a record's status as active or inactive. All jobs open to labor or still billable to the client are considered active. These active records are housed within the SOM office. Correspondence is coded and sent immediately to the Central File Department. Graphics are retained by the project team until the job is completed. Accounting records and models are housed in their respective departments, both within close proximity to Central File.

Once a job closes and the project is completed, all related records take on inactive status. Correspondence is boxed by the Central File staff and sent to a dead storage warehouse. Graphics are rolled or boxed by a project team member and sent to Central File. The Archivist then separates architectural drawings and specifications for microfilming and forwards everything to dead storage. Accounting Department and Model Shop, likewise, prepare their specific materials for the warehouse.

Use

Project team members and their secretaries are the primary users of SOM's Central File. Retrieval of pertinent correspondence of contracts fill the information voids of their various projects. Drawings of previous jobs serve as examples for future alterations. Legal questions are answered by forwarding accounting files to SOM's attorneys. Background and current status of every SOM project can be and is researched by the Central File user.

OPERATING PROCEDURES

All SOM offices have found the need for standardizing their operating procedures on every level. This practice has been extremely helpful in the organization and operation of the Central File Department. All procedural practices are in writing, available to all personnel and periodically updated to fit SOM's ever-changing administrative environment.

Control of Records

Accurate control of records is the main goal of Central File. This is best accomplished by strict adherence to the following items:

— file manual
— file index
— classification systems.

The *SOM New York File Manual* is a document produced by the Central File Department, annually updated and distributed to all project managers and their secretaries. In keeping with the SOM team philosophy, the File Manual must be reviewed by a committee before changes can be approved. This document serves as a manual of Central File practices and use. It describes, in detail, the purpose and organization of the department and provides a step-by-step orientation for the user. The File Manual includes special instructions for opening a job number, preparing documents for filing and storage, coding and use of the File Index, retrieval, retention, etc. (see Figure 1).

The File Index is the core of Central File's organization of records. This unique system serves as both a guide for the coding of documents and a record of what is contained in a project file.

Each job open to labor has its own file and billing number. The first item included in each new job file is the File Index Sheet which contains an outline of the classification scheme for that project. As correspondence accumulates, it is coded according to this outline and corresponding classification numbers are circled on the sheet before filing. This way it is possible to see what types of correspondence are available for each job. When the project is nearing completion and graphics and other records are prepared for the warehouse, Inactive Storage Forms are completed and added to the file (see Figure 2). This way the history of every job can be seen at a glance.

SOM NEW YORK FILE MANUAL

(sample section)

Coding and Use of File Index

    A. Responsibility for Coding

        It is the sole responsibility of the Project Manager to correctly code all correspondence before sending it to Central File.

        If uncoded material is received in Central File it will be returned for coding.

    B. File Index Sheet

        The File Index sheet serves two purposes: 1) It is a guide for the coding of documents; 2) It is Central File's record of what is contained in a project file.

        When notification of a new project is received, the File Supervisor enters the information on the top of the Index Sheet and places it alphabetically in the CURRENT JOB FILE, which contains a similar sheet for each active project. As material is sent to Central File, the class number of the file is circled on the sheet to indicate that a file on that subject exists. Files are not opened in anticipation of material to be received.

Figure 1

INACTIVE STORAGE FORM

Figure 2

PROJECT NAME	PROJECT #	MICROFILM #	DESCRIPTION OF DOCUMENTS	SIGNATURE	DATE TO STORAGE	LOCATION

The classification schemes that make up the File Index are quite complex. The original system was based on a series of three-digit numbers, the main classes being, 100, 200, etc. with subdivisions of 110, 120, etc. For example, "Site" becomes a subdividison of "Design" in the following breakdown:

200 Design
   210 Interior
   220 Site
   230 Architectural, etc.

While this system worked well initially, projects became larger and correspondence increased tremendously, making the existing subheadings obsolete. As technology also changed, new terminologies followed new techniques and a second, more detailed classification system was devised. This second system, based on a four-digit series of numbers offers extra sub-groupings for a more complex information need. For example, "Site" becomes a main class in the following breakdown:

2000 Site
   210 Site Survey/Mapping
   220 Subsurface Investigation
   230 Excavation/Foundation, etc.

Because of the massive amount of records in storage and the successful acceptance of the first coding system, a retrospective conversion has been unnecessary.

One outstanding feature of SOM's classification system relates back to the Firm's team concept. Here is a rare example of a user-created system. A committee was formed to study various existing architectural classification schemes and draw from them in the development of a unique coding method. The result is a system flexible enough for a large volume of records as well as the intricacies of a complex subject matter.

While the File Index is Central File's major tool for the organization of active records, a computer-printed Inactive Records List has proven indispensable for control of dead storage items. Active records make up a small part of SOM's files and, as such, can be physically accessed rather easily. However, the large amount of dead files, coupled with limited availability of storage space require a random-access system of shelving. Also as older records are destroyed and new items added, a computer-printed shelf-list is vital (see Figure 3).

Retrieval

In order to retrieve a document from active records, the user should supply as much information as possible: job name and number, classification number, type of record, approximate date, etc. Items may be removed for copying or borrowed for a reasonable length of time. No documents should be retrieved or refiled by anyone other than Central File personnel. Turnaround time for borrowing active records is usually immediate.

When recalling material from inactive records, the same guidelines for retrieving active records should be followed. However, since the storage facility is at another location, sufficient travel time must be allowed for. Small amounts of files and drawings, which can be pulled readily by the Archivist, usually have a same-day turnaround time. However, removal of boxes of correspondence, large rolled drawings or models require assistance from warehouse personnel, requiring at least one or two days advance notice.

Microfilming

Because of the slow turnaround time for retrieval of inactive records, a system of microfilming was instituted at SOM. Microfilming assures that important, though inactive, information is readily available in the office. Microfilms of architectural drawings and specifications are available to the user for viewing and printing. Drawings are filmed on 35mm film, which can be utilized on the reader/printer in the Central File office. Specifications, filmed on 16mm film, can be viewed and copied on a machine in the nearby Specification Department. Whenever possible, microfilm is referred to instead of original documents.

DESTRUCTION/WEEDING OF MATERIALS

Skidmore, Owings and Merrill has experienced a steady growth since its inception in 1936. The increased number of clients and projects has led to an overwhelming accumulation of records. This,

COMPUTER-PRINTED SHELF-LIST

(sample section)

Shelf Location	Destroy Date	Title, Job Name, Job Number & Description of Contents
1345	1987	Estimating Files: Astoria Film Studios thru Seagram Bldg, May 20, 1981 (1 of 2).
1346	1990	Texaco #3734: Shop Drawings, Mechanical, Plumbing, Ductwork, 1976.
1347	1990	Texaco #3734: Shop Drawings, 15400 thru 16100, 1975.
1348	1992	Accounting: Paid Vouchers, F.Y. 1982, National Blueprint.
1349	1986	Otis Elevator #2616: Shop Drawings 5, 8, 10, 1974.
1350	1987	Baren Files: Olympic Tower, Corres., Invoices, 1971-76.
1351	1995	Georgia Pacific #1285: C.F. 275-291.
1352	1995	Georgia Padific #1285: C.F. 305-308.
1353	Hold	Chase Manhattan Bank #677, 620E, 623E, 671: NY Plaza, CMB-Met Branch Bank, 1960-64.

Figure 3

coupled with a sudden shortage of available storage space, has put special emphasis on the need for weeding and ultimate destruction of older materials.

Retention Policies

Although written SOM retention policies have existed for some time, only recently have efforts been made to update, standardize and enforce them. Let us examine the current policies for the various types of Central File records.

Printed records have a varied retention period. Correspondence is retained ten years after job completion, then destroyed. Specifications are microfilmed and originals discarded after microfilm accuracy has been assured. Estimating files have a two-year review period and are destroyed at the discretion of the department head. Contract files are considered important enough to remain permanently. Although a project was begun for microfilming of older contracts, it was later abandoned for not being cost-effective.

Retention schedules for graphics have been revised recently. The various types of preliminary design drawings, detail drawings, sketches, presentation flats, photos, etc., once had indefinite retention periods. Now, all miscellaneous drawings have the same destruction schedule as shop drawings, which is ten years after job closing. All architectural drawings, also called working drawings, are microfilmed and the rolled originals held permanently in storage.

Accounting records have extremely complex and equally strict retention schedules. In a recent restructuring of destruction timetables, nearly forty accounting sub-groups which previously had indefinite retention status were standardized. Payroll registers, job distribution, general ledger and personnel files are among the limited number of items now held permanently. Invoices, paid vouchers, cancelled checks, petty cash receipts, commission registers, client master list, etc. are retained for ten years. Order books, check registers, check books, budget and fee analyses, time cards and other similar records are discarded after six years.

Models, as well as samples and other presentation material, are subject to periodic review and destroyed only upon approval. The enormous cost of the making of models, in terms of both materials and man-hours, makes the decision for destruction a difficult one. Before a model is discarded, attempts are made to send it to the client, display it at SOM, donate it to a museum, school or library, or to return it to the Model Shop for mismantling and reuse.

Gaining Approval for Destruction

When the retention period of any material has expired, approval for its destruction is sought by the File Supervisor. If approval is not granted, the material is reviewed every year until it can be destroyed. No material can be destroyed by Central File personnel without proper authorization.

At the time a record is sent to dead storage, a destruction date is set and included as an entry in the computer-printed Inactive Records List. An annual review for destruction begins with each new calendar year and the shelf list is sorted to produce a list of expired materials. To facilitate speedy approval, a Destruction Approval List is circulated to the appropriate partners and project mangers. This list compartmentalizes the following information: storage location, job name and number, brief description of documents, date of materials, date of job completion, project team members and person responsible for destruction approval (see Figure 4).

Preparation for Destruction

When the Destruction Approval List is initialled by the appropriate partners and returned to Central File, the preparation for destruction begins. Records which have not received approval are given a new, usually next year, destruction date. A list of remaining items, in shelf list order, is given to the Archivist who makes a reservation for two or more warehouse personnel, who physically discard the approved boxes, rolls and models. These items are deleted from the Inactive Records List and the initialled Destruction Approval List is kept for future reference.

Problems

While destruction/weeding of materials at SOM is recognized as a vital Central File project and approached conscientiously and systematically, problems still arise even in the most organized of environments.

Accounting records pose a particular problem in the area of standardization of terminology. For example, is a "journal

DESTRUCTION APPROVAL LIST

(sample section)

Shelf	Job Name	Job #	Materials	Date	Closing	Team	Approval
0426	BANQUE LAMBERT	1708	Corres., s.d., equip files, cuts, etc.	1959-64	1965	Bunshaft, Gans, Overcash	Bailey
0427							
0687							
0423	BEEKMAN HOSPITAL	0275	Prod. files, corres., trans., s.d., repts, etc.	1967-69	1972	Cutler, Olson, Goodman	Bailey
0424							
0428							
0429							
0430							
0703	BLUE HILL PROJECT	0604	S.D.	1968-71	1974	Severinghaus, Hughes	Bailey
0704							
0706							
0707							

Figure 4

JOURNAL. *LINN*EAN *SOC*IETY OF LONDON
JOURNAL DE *MICR*OSCOPIE
JOURNAL OF *MICR*OSCOPY

In order to aid customers to locate the periodicals under this arrangement, the librarians provide information sheets describing the format. The staff members post a list on each range of shelves indicating those titles shelved in that particular range. They add information to the in-house location file, noting the title under which the periodical is shelved by underscoring the first word in red ink. They mark each volume with a white dot, indicating that it is a periodical, and underscore the first word of the title in white to aid the student shelvers to place the volumes correctly.

However, the undergraduates, faculty, research staff, and customers complain still that they cannot find the journals. They are unable to walk to the shelves to find a reference in J. BIOL. CHEM. as JOURNAL OF *BIO*LOGICAL *CHEM*ISTRY. Some library staff members have difficulty tracing changes of title in the microfiche serials list. However, most of them learn quickly to locate the titles on the shelves.

The reasons for failure seem to be a combination of personal problems, cataloging and system management problems, and local errors. Many of these factors apply also to collections in the social sciences and humanities.

PERSONAL PROBLEMS

— People are accustomed to the old filing rules that journals are filed according to the corporate entry, such as, AMERICAN CHEMICAL SOCIETY. JOURNAL.
— Customers are not acquainted with foreign languages. They have difficulty with various words in different languages, such as:

annals, annalen, annales
bulletin, boletin, boletim
journal of, journal de, zhurnal
revista, rivista
review, revue

They have difficulty tracing changes of title, even those which involve minor changes. ZEITSCHRIFT FUR PARASITENKUNDE. PARASITOLOGIC RESEARCH changed to ZEITSCHRIFT FUR PARASITKUNDE. PARASITOLOGY RESEARCH, but the abbreviation remains the same—Z. PARASITKD.

- People were not forced to memorize the alphabet when they attended elementary school.
- Customers cannot determine from the title if the publication is a periodical or a serial or a monograph. The titles which commence with the words "Advances," "Progress," or "Reviews" always are difficult to identify. ACTA HORTICULTURAE is cited as if it is a journal, but, in the Purdue Libraries, it is cataloged as a monograph. People look for AGRONOMY ABSTRACTS in the abstract area. It is shelved with the serials and monographs because it is composed of the abstracts of the papers presented at the annual meeting of the American Society of Agronomy, the Soil Science Society of America, and the Crop Science Society of America. JOURNAL OF THE SPORTS TURF RESEARCH INSTITUTE, which is published annually, is shelved with the serials and monographs.
- Customers are not aware of the frequency of publication for serials. When the frequency changes, according to the definition above, the titles are moved from serials to periodicals or vice versa. An example is ANNUAL REPORT OF THE QUEBEC SOCIETY FOR THE PROTECTION OF PLANTS which is continued by PHYTOPROTECTION.
- Authors sometimes do not cite a title correctly. When there is a change of title, they are confused whether it should be listed as SIGMA XI QUARTERLY volume 30 no. 1, 1942 or AMERICAN SCIENTIST volume 30 no. 1, 1942.

Cataloging and System Management Problems

- Research is interdisciplinary, but the various abstract services and style manuals do not cite titles in the same format. In addition, customers request journals by their "popular" names. PROCEEDINGS OF THE NATIONAL ACADEMY OF SCIENCES is listed as PROC NAT ACAD SCI USA in both CASSI and BIOSIS. However, the biologists request it by the CODEN, which is PNAS.

— Some of the abbreviations cannot be used because they are not compatible with the OCLC entries. BIOSIS gives the title as COMPTES RENDUS HEBDOMADAIRES DES SEANCES DE L'ACADEMIE DES SCIENCES with the abbreviation C R HEBD SEANCES ACAD SCI. Since the OCLC entry is COMPTES RENDUS DES SEANCES DE L'ACADEMIE DES SCIENCES, we shelve the title as COMPT REND. Another example is that BIOSIS omits the "CRC" prefix from the abbreviation for titles, but OCLC includes it in the entries. BIOSIS uses the abbreviation CRIT REV BIOCHEM for CRC CRITICAL REVIEWS IN BIOCHEMISTRY. Currently we shelve the title under "CRC."
— There are errors in the OCLC records. OCLC lists the final volume of TROPICAL ABSTRACTS as v. 28, 1973, while the final volume actually is v. 29, 1974.
— The periodicals which change title then revert to the former title become a burden to trace both in the microfiche and on the shelves. An example is RECLAMATION RECORD

continued by NEW RECLAMATION ERA
continued by RECLAMATION ERA (1932)
continued by WATER AND POWER ERA
continued by RECLAMATION ERA (1981)

— Similarly, divisions in titles become too complex to follow, such as:

JOURNAL OF THE LINNEAN SOCIETY OF LONDON. BOTANY
continued by BOTANICAL JOURNAL OF THE LINNEAN SOCIETY

— The cataloging rules include nuances which are incomprehensible to the lay person. An example is the separate entries for titles which include the ampersand, such as:

SOIL & WATER CONSERVATION
SOIL AND WATER CONSERVATION

Another example is a separate entry for titles for which there are holdings both as paper copy and microform. There are two entries for DROVERS JOURNAL, which is retained at Pur-

due in paper copy about two years until the microfilm is received.
— The periodicals which change title in the midst of a volume often have been bound under the most recent title. In order to guide people to two titles which are bound in the same physical volume, the library staff members insert notes in the location files, notes on the shelves, etc. An example is

GREAT LAKES ENTOMOLOGIST v. 5 includes v. 2-4 of
MICHIGAN ENTOMOLOGIST

The corresponding record is

MICHIGAN ENTOMOLOGIST v. 2-4 bound in v. 5 of
GREAT LAKES ENTOMOLOGIST

However, this information is not yet included in the microfiche serials record.
— The format of the microfiche serials record is that titles are listed under all possible entries. Customers must be instructed to look in the subject or the shelf list portions of the fiche or in the local files in order to find the entry under which the title is shelved in the Life Sciences Library.
— For more than two years the titles which had not yet been converted to OCLC were kept in a separate section of the microfiche serials records. These titles were alphabetized under rules that were different from those used for the converted titles.
— The listings in the microfiche do not indicate which titles are shelved as periodicals and which as serials. This information has been inserted in the fiche commencing in 1982 and currently covers less than half the periodicals in the Life Sciences Library.
— Only a portion of the titles have been converted to AACR2. The microfiche serials list currently represents several different cataloging rules. Even those titles which were converted several years ago are being revised again when the catalogers find the AACR2 entries in the OCLC data base.
— The titles which have not been converted are shelved in the Life Sciences Library according to the individual titles under which they have been published. However, the journals are

listed in all other records in the library system only under their most recent titles; often the cross-references have disappeared from the microfiche record.
— The standard location designator in the microfiche for periodicals is "Periodicals Room." Life Sciences Library does not have a periodicals room but a periodicals area on the main and fourth floors.
— The microfiche serials list still contains obsolete location designators, such as, "Warehouse" or "4th floor storage" or "Attic." People assume erroneously that the latter two refer to the fourth floor or attic of Lilly Hall, the building in which the Life Sciences Library is located.
— The shelf list portion of the fiche includes the complete bibliographic record. People have difficulty distinguishing between the volumes that have been published and those that the library system owns. An example is

KYOTO DAIGAKU. NOGAKUBU. MEMOIRS OF THE COLLEGE OF AGRICULTURE, KYOTO UNIVERSITY. no. 1, 1926-
   Life 104-113, 1973-1979

— The AACR2 entries for non-Roman alphabet titles are the transliterated titles with the English sub-title. An example is given above. However, the foreign language titles which have not yet been converted to AACR2 remain cataloged under different rules. Since the customers are not aware of the conversion project, they become very much confused when looking for Chinese or Japanese journal titles.

LOCAL ERRORS

— The library staff members have made errors in binding, such as binding titles under an obsolete title or combining two titles in the same volume before the catalog department issued corrections. Many of these errors, which existed for a number of years, surfaced only when the titles were alphabetized.
— The records indicate the volumes that are in storage are incomplete and sometimes inaccurate.
— The staff members continuously are correcting the alphabeti-

zation due to errors made in the 1981 move or changes brought about by the conversion project.
— A problem both for the public service and the catalog departments is to note all of the titles under which a periodical was published when making changes in locations, changes in holdings, or changes in cataloging. A simple transfer of 10 volumes to storage requires three separate forms due to changes of title. This situation only compounds the chances for errors.
— Since OCLC has not programmed an automatic notification for changes in titles, the library system must depend upon the serials assistants and subject specialists to notify the catalogers of revisions. In practice, these may remain unnoticed for months due to the pressure of other work.
— Since the filing rules were not available in 1981 in the Life Sciences Library, the journals are not shelved in the same order as the entries in the microfiche. The primary error is that initials are shelved at the beginning of each letter instead of being interfiled in alphabetical order. This final adjustment to the alphabetization will be scheduled late in 1985 when the OCLC conversion is completed.

CONCLUSION

In conclusion, we have found that the intent of AACR2 to simplify identifying periodical titles has not proven to be successful in our situation. There are many factors inherent to serials and periodicals, as Pinzelik[8] and Murfin[9] mention, which do not relate to AACR2. Many times these involve publishers' decisions to change titles in the midst of a volume, suspend publication, or cease, combine, or supersede titles. The various abstracting and indexing services do not use the same abbreviation for a title. The OCLC entry may not match the BIOSIS or CASSI abbreviation. The authors do not always record references either in a standard format or accurately. The customers do not always record the citations correctly. Many times there are errors in binding volumes or recording holdings in the libraries. The entries in the microfiche serials records may provide too much information or too little information for the customer to locate the periodical easily.[10]

Conversion projects, due to financial and staff resources that are available, must span several years. This means that, during the project, the serials records represent several versions of the cataloging rules and several location designators. Each periodical title must be treated as a separate problem whenever a customer asks for assistance.

McCarthy[11] and Farber[12] mention that instructing people in library use only heightens their expectations to find material without assistance. Customers who regularly use a collection usually can learn to find the journals which are pertinent to them. However, Soules[13] states, in discussing monographs, that

> . . . The user cannot cope when we provide something that appears to have no consistent pattern, especially when that inconsistency is compounded by our inability to cope retrospectively, leaving us half in and out of two sets of rules . . .

TITLES WHICH ARE MENTIONED

Acta Horticulturae. 1963- . The Hague, Netherlands: International Society for Horticultural Science.

Agronomy Abstracts. v. 1- . 1949- . Madison, WI: American Society of Agronomy.

American Chemical Society. *Journal of the American Chemical Society.* v. 1- . 1879- . Washington, DC.

Comptes Rendus des Seances de L'Academie des Sciences. Serie III. Sciences de la Vie. T. 292, ser. III, no. 1 (5 Jan. 1981) - . Paris: Gauthier-Villars, c1981- .

CRC Critical Reviews in Biochemistry. v. 1- . 1973- . Boca Raton, FL: CRC Press.

Chicago Daily Farmers' and Drovers' Journal. 18___-1917. Chicago, IL: Drovers Journal Publishing Co. Continued by *Chicago Daily Drovers Journal* 1917-1960. Continued by *Drover's Journal.* v. 89- . 1961- .

Journal of the Proceedings of the Linnean Society. Botany. v. 1-7, 1855-1864. Continued by *Journal of the Linnean Society of London. Botany.* v. 8-61, 1865-1968. *Botanical Journal of the Linnean Society.* v. 62- . 1969- .

Kyoto Daigaku. Negakubu. Memoirs of the College of Agriculture, Kyoto University. no. 1- . 1926- .

Michigan Entomologist. v. 1-4, July 1966-Winter 1971. East Lansing MI: Michigan Entomological Society. Continued by *Great Lakes Entomologist,* v. 5- . Spring 1972- .

Proceedings of the National Academy of Sciences of the United States of America. v. 1-76, 1915-1979. Washington, DC: National Academy of Sciences. Continued by *Proceedings of the National Academy of Sciences of the United States of America. Biological Sciences* v. 77- . 1980- . and by *Proceedings of the National Academy of Sciences of the United States of America. Physical Sciences* v. 77- . 1980- .

Reclamation Record. v. 1-15, 1908-1924. Washington, DC: Bureau of Reclamation. Continued by *New Reclamation Era* v. 15-22, 1924-1931. Continued by *Reclamation Era (1932)* v. 23-65, 1932-1979. Washington, DC: Water and Power Resources Service, U.S. Department of the Interior. Continued by *Water and Power Era* v. 66 no. 1, 1981. Continued by *Reclamation Era (1981)* v. 66 no. 2, 1981- v. 67, 1983. Washington: Bureau of Reclamation.

Societe de Quebec pour la Protection des Plantes contre les Insectes et les Plantes Parasites. Rapport Annuel. v. 1, 1908-1909. Continued by *Quebec Society for the Protection of Plants from Insects and Fungous Diseases. Annual Report* v. 2-12, 1909-1920. Continued by *Quebec Society for the Protection of Plants. Annual Report* v. 13-43, 1920-1961. Continued by *Phytoprotection* v. 44- . 1963- . Quebec: Ministere de l'Agriculture et de la Colonisation.

Sigma Xi Quarterly v. 1 (March 1913)- v. 30 no. 1 (January 1942). Champaign, IL: Society of the Sigma Xi. Continued by *American Scientist* v. 30 no. 2, April 1942- . New Haven, CT: Sigma Xi.

Soil & Water Conservation News. v. 1 no. 1 (April 1980)- v. 2 no. 3 (June 1981). Washington, DC: U.S. Department of Agriculture. Soil Conservation Service. Continued by *Soil and Water Conservation News* v. 2 no. 4, July 1981- .

Sports Turf Research Institute, Bingley, Yorkshire. Journal of the Sports Turf Research Institute. v. 1- . 1929- .

Tropical Abstracts. v. 1-29, 1946-1974. Amsterdam: Royal Tropical Institute.

Zeitschrift fur Parasitenkunde. Parasitologic Research. Bd. 1-55, 1928-1977. Berlin: Springer Verlag. Superseded by *Zeitschrift fur Parasitenkunde. Parasitology Research.* v. 56- . 1978- .

REFERENCES

1. Pinzelik, Barbara P. The serials maze: providing public service for a large serials collection. *Journal of Academic Librarianship.* 8 (2): 89-94; 1981.

2. Murfin, Marjorie E. The myth of accessibility: frustration and failure in retrieving periodicals. *Journal of Academic Librarianship.* 6 (1): 16-19; 1980.

3. Adapted from the definition of "Periodical" in L. M. Harrod's *Librarians' Glossary,* 4th rev. ed., Westview, 1977, p. 633.

4. Purdue is using a plan similar to the one described by Ruth B. McBride in "Copy cataloguing of serials according to AACR2 using OCLC: the University of Illinois experience." *In: The management of serials automation.* Edited by Peter Gellatly. New York: Haworth Press; 1982: 135-150 (A monographic supplement to the *Serials Librarian* 6 (1981/1982).

5. Cole, Jim E. Unique serial title entries. *Serials Review.* 75: 75; 1981 Oct./Dec.

6. *Chemical Abstracts Service Source Index.* 1970- . Columbus, OH, American Chemical Society. This is commonly referred to as CASSI.

7. *Serial Sources for the BIOSIS Data Base.* 1978- . Philadelphia, PA: BioSciences Information Service, 1979- .

8. Pinzelik, op cit.

9. Murfin, op cit.

10. These and other factors are discussed by Barbara Pinzelik in "The periodical, the patron, and AACR2" *In: AACR2 and Serials: the American View.* Edited by Neal Edgar. New York: Haworth Press; 1983: 41-45. Another discussion is found in Terrence J. O'Malley. Union listing via OCLC's serials control subsystem. *Special Libraries.* 75(2): 131-150; 1984 Apr.

11. McCarthy, Constance. Library instruction: observations from the reference desk. *RQ* 22: 36-41; 1982 Fall.

12. Farber, Evan Ira. Catalog dependency. *Library Journal.* 109 (3): 325-328; 1984 Feb. 15

13. Soule, Aline. The deterioration of quality cataloging. *Library Journal.* 108 (1): 27-29; 1983 Jan 1.

SCI-TECH COLLECTIONS

Tony Stankus, Editor

Frank Kellerman's current paper presents our readers with at least three notable features. First, it is in tune with a tremendously important social and scientific problem. Even though this manuscript will appear some time after popular awareness has peaked, scholarly and policy-making interest will continue for what is hopefully a long enough time to deal with the issues meaningfully. Second, in light of this paper's special timeliness, and with the courteous cooperation of other contributors who have held their manuscripts in abeyance, it has been decided that this will be the first repeat authorship in our series. (See *STL* volume 5, number 2, "Artificial Internal Organs: Brief Guide to the Research and Literature" for our colleague's initial work.) Third, Kellerman's is one of the most thoroughgoing papers in its exposition of a problem of information handling ethics: the shakiness of data in a critical situation. While Kellerman offers no clear cut answers on whether or not librarians should disseminate it in every circumstance, he suggests that we as professionals have some duty to inform clientele about credibility, basing our warning on a close examination of just how the information was gathered prior to its publication.

Malnutrition and Disease in the Third World: Sources and Reliability of the Statistics

Frank R. Kellerman

ABSTRACT. Malnutrition and disease are chronic problems in the Third World. It is difficult to find reliable statistical information that accurately describes the conditions. Problems with the statistics are discussed and statistics sources are presented. Then, specific diseases are noted and the literature covering the diseases follows.

MULTIPLE PERSPECTIVES AND MULTIPLE PROBLEMS

The drought and famine in Ethiopia this past year have once again brought to our attention the scope of suffering in areas in the Third World. There are two important points that should be made: this famine is certainly not the first in the area (there was a severe famine in Ethiopia in 1972), and, even without the famine, there is a chronic situation of malnourishment and disease that will continue to demand the attention of scholars and policymakers.

The discussions of the problems and solutions for droughts and famines involve many disciplines. Meteorology needs to be considered, because of the weather and drought conditions. The agricultural situation is studied to determine the capacity of food production. Biology and medicine are brought in to determine the nutritional needs of the population and the provision of health care. Economics determines the ability of the country and individuals to purchase adequate food. Political science/government plays a large part in determining the distribution of resources and handling the regula-

---

Frank R. Kellerman is Biomedical Reference Librarian, Brown University, Sciences Library, Box I, Providence, RI 02912. He has a BA degree from the University of Michigan and the MSLS degree from Case Western Reserve University.

tions that either facilitate or hinder aid to the country. The sociological/cultural and anthropological aspects of life in the country are other factors that must be dealt with. All of these approaches require statistical information. Many of the resultant reports generate even more statistics.

We often hear accounts about the numbers of people dying each month or each day from the famine. Yet, an important question that needs to be answered is how many people were already dying each month or each day from malnourishment or diseases exacerbated by malnutrition even without the presence of this particular famine. This is not to minimize the effects of the present crisis. It is more to acknowledge the ongoing problem and the need for information to address the problem. Consider the following. The 1982 U.N. *Report on the world social situation* notes that:

> Global estimates of the number of people in hunger vary according to the nutritional standard adopted and the assumptions made about the distribution of food consumption within countries and within households. They range from a figure of 100 million, obtained by applying a restrictive, clinical definition of hunger, to as large a figure as 500 million. The latest estimate from the Food and Agriculture Organization of the United Nations shows the number who do not get a sufficient diet as at least 430 million.[1]

But what do these numbers mean? How is malnutrition measured? Can it be measured for a population? Are numbers available that adequately portray the health of a population?

It is difficult to obtain accurate statistics for vital, social, and even economic measurements of the Third World countries in the best of times. How then could we obtain reliable numbers on the people who are in peril from a famine? The answer, it seems, is that we cannot. Even the statistics that we can find on seemingly more clear cut measures, e.g., the number of births, are not dependable. When it comes to a quantification of the number who are malnourished, finding reliable numbers is even less likely. R. V. Garcia and J. C. Escudero have studied the 1927 drought/famine in Ethiopia and concluded among other things:

> Other recommendations within this order of feasibility are related to the failure of the conventional health statistics system

to monitor the extent of malnutrition and of other diseases in the population, to ascertain their chronic level or the increase in them as the drought takes hold. The tremendous under-registration of vital events—births, deaths and their causes—make vital statistics very bad indicators of the health of the population, and the fact that the system as it exists is heavily biased towards recording events which occur in urban areas—which are in turn not only unrepresentative of countries that are mostly rural, but are also biased against malnutrition—make any extrapolation on their findings seem even harmful if the objective is to arrive at a nationwide determination of health problems.[2]

How accurate are the collected statistics? The *Demographic Yearbook* of the U.N. has vital statistics for over "200 countries or areas." The numbers published in it are obtained from surveys sent out by the U.N. Statistical Office and filled in by national statistical bureaus of those countries/areas. The reported numbers are graded for probable accuracy. However, for the most part, it is the country that is reporting that also supplies the judgement about accuracy. In 1977, the U.N. included a question asking on what basis the country made that determination on accuracy. As yet (1982 Yearbook), the countries, for the most part, have not chosen to fill in that portion of the questionnaire.

Many international agencies collect numbers and publish them. The United Nations, the World Bank, and the Food and Agriculture Organization of the U.N. are a few of the most prominent. These organizations may be able to collect some statistics directly and may do some manipulations of the statistics they receive in order to make comparisons between countries. However, the vast majority of the statistics that they have to work with are obtained from reports given out by the individual countries. The quality of the statistics varies from country to country.

What are some of the problems with these numbers? (The *Demographic Yearbook*[3] elaborates on the following points.)

1. *Definitions.* There may not be a standardized definition of a phenomenon or it may not be used. There would be a wide variability of the division of what is urban and what is rural, for example. However, there are also discrepancies in report-

ing live births. In some places, a baby dying after a few hours is often not reported as a live birth.

2. *Registering of vital events.* Many countries have mandatory registration of these events, but it may apply, in practice, to only certain groups or nationalities within the country.

3. *Dates.* For comparison between countries, the date of the occurrence of an event is needed. Often the date of reporting of the event instead of occurrence will be the date registered.

4. *Causes of death.* For causes of death, the International Classification of Disease (ICD-9) is used to standardize the information. Often, nonmedical personnel assign the cause of death. The errors from this represent alot of underclassification of causes of death from some diseases and overclassification from others.

5. *Incomplete information.* In many cases, the reported information supplied by the country is not complete. At this point, estimates are given either by the country or by the international agency. And as the *Demographic Yearbook* stated in regard to one area: ". . . because of their estimated character, these distributions by broad age groups and sex should be considered only as orders of magnitude."[4]

6. *Age groups errors.* The skepticism toward the statistics grows when it is noticed that seemingly straightforward numbers such as age groups are obviously not correct. It is often found that there is an overrepresentation of people with ages ending in a "0" or a "5." In fact, there is a "Whipple's Index" to check for this phenomenon in the reported numbers.

7. *Evaluation of the data.* Some of these compilations of statistics like the *Demographic Yearbook* seem forthcoming in noting the pitfalls of the statistics listed. There are ample introductory remarks and footnotes to give warning. However, with the *Demographic Yearbook,* it should be noted that it relies on the reporting country to some extent to give an estimation of the completeness of its vital data, because " . . . it was felt that national statistical offices were in the best position to judge the quality of their data."[5]

8. *Duplication.* Some of these statistics compendiums will reproduce numbers gotten from the compendiums. For example, the *World Health Statistics Annual* takes part of its numbers from the *Demographic Yearbook*. Therefore, the appearance of a particular quantity over and over again in the

sources may not indicate verification. It may mean repetition of an error.
9. *Statistics for malnutrition.* Are there really numbers that would help us understand the problem of malnutrition? For instance, a publication of the World Bank called *World tables* has numbers for "protein supply per capita (grams per day)" and "calorie supply per capita (percentage of requirements)." These numbers appear useful, but do not show the food distribution problems. For famines, it may often be the case that there is not a shortage of food, but a lack of purchasing power. Often, less direct measures may be more adequate in judging the health of a population. M. Morris uses a "Physical Quality of Life Index (PQLI)."[6] In a publication studying the conditions of the Sahel, Morris et al. state: " . . . indicators should measure the net results obtained from the Plan rather than inputs, and they should reflect the distribution of results among significant groups in the population."[7] The PQLI includes infant mortality, life expectancy at age 1, and basic literacy. One still needs to use the given data, but these numbers should be more reliable than the "protein per capita" type of numbers.

SORTING OUT THE SOURCES

The last section's aim was to act as a warning about the unreliability of the reported statistics. This section presents the publications which have those statistics. A summary of the vital/health statistics for the major publications discussed below (numbers 1-8) is presented in Figure 1. Several sources may use the same terms, e.g., fertility rate. The definition used by one source may not be exactly the same as the definition from another source.

Statistics—Sources—Handy Reference Publications

1. Demographic Yearbook

This annual publication is a convenient source for vital statistics. Besides giving the year's statistics, each volume includes a cumulated subject index for volume one on to the present volume. This is helpful, because each volume has special subjects covered, in addition to the statistics presented every year.

	DEM	STA	WHO	WDR	WBT	ENC	WPO	FAO
Population	x	x	x	x	x	x	x	x
Gener.Mortality Rate	x	x	x	x	x	x	x	
Child Mortality Rate	x			x	x	x		
Infant Mortality Rate	x	x	x	x	x	x	x	
Causes of Death	x		x					
Life Expectancy	x	x	x	x	x	x	x	
Birth Rate	x	x	x	x	x	x	x	
Fertility Rate	x	x		x	x	x		
Natural Increase	x	x	x			x		
Death Rate Decline				x		x		
Morbidity			x					
Physicians Per Cap.		x		x	x	x		
Nurs.Pers.Per Cap.				x	x			
Hospital Beds Per Cap.		x			x	x		
Calories Per Cap.				x	x	x		
Protein Per Cap.					x	x		
Food Prod.Per Cap.				x		x		x
Food Production		x		x		x		x
Land Use						x		x
Literacy					x	x	x	
PQLI						x		
Marriage Rate	x	x				x		
Divorce Rate	x	x				x		

Figure 1. Handy Reference Publications
Demographic Yearbook = DEM
Statistical Yearbook = STA
World Health Statistics Annual = WHO
World Tables = WBT
World Development Report = WDR
Encyclopedia of the Third World = ENC
FAO Production Yearbook = FAO
World Population = WPO

2. Statistical Yearbook[8]

This yearbook has an emphasis more on the economic statistics than the vital statistics. It does, however, have a useful collection of vital/health statistics.

3. World Health Statistics Annual[9]

There are some statistics in this that are taken directly from the *Demographic Yearbook*. In addition, the *World Health Statistics Annual* has detailed statistics for countries on morbidity and mortality. Starting with the 1984 edition, the morbidity for diptheria, measles, pertussis, poliomyelitis, tetanus, and tuberculosis. The bulk of the *Annual* has the tabular information on causes of death. Most of the current edition uses the ICD-9. There are tables by country for "causes of death, by sex and age" and "causes of infant death, by sex and age."

4. World Development Report[10]

Like the *Statistical Yearbook*, this has a lot of economic information, but is also a good source for selected vital/health related statistics. In addition to those annual tables, there are charts and graphs throughout the *Report* on other issues of interest, e.g., trends in contraceptive use.

5. World Tables[11]

v.II—social data (v.I is the economic data).
"The primary sources for data in these tables are the publications of specialized international agencies, such as UNESCO, FAO, WHO, ILO, and the U.N. Statistical Office; they are supplemented by data from the World Bank data files."[12] So, although much of the data appears elsewhere, this is a convenient source. For example, turn to the pages for a specific country. Under this, find the section, "Health and Nutrition." Under this section, there are numbers for "population per physician," "population per nursing person," "population per hospital bed," "calorie supply per capita (percentage of requirements)," "protein supply per capita (grams per day)," "infant mortality rate," and "child (1-4) death rate."

6. Encyclopedia of the Third World[13]

This is a convenient, readable source of information. Each country has a paragraph or two for subjects ranging from the legal system to food. Some of the vital statistics given are crude death rate, life expectancy at birth, infant mortality rate, and child death rate. The Physical Quality of Life Index number is also given. This publication also has a word concerning the statistics: "Data on less developed countries are subject to numerous qualifications and are only intended as approximations and estimates rather than as precise or unquestionable data."[14]

7. World Population[15]

This publication gives two pages of information on each country. The countries are arranged alphabetically under the appropriate continent.

8. FAO Production Yearbook[16]

This is the publication to check for agricultural production in each country. Numbers are given for both broad areas of agriculture, e.g., cereals, and for specific crops, e.g., linseed. There are also numbers for per capita agricultural production.

Other useful sources that are not in Figure 1:

9. World Factbook[17]

This publication is arranged alphabetically by country with two pages of information, mostly statistical, devoted to each country. Numbers given that may be relevant for the purpose of health are population, literacy, and labor force.

10. World Bank Atlas[18]

This small publication gives GNP numbers and population with growth rates.

11. Population and Vital Statistics Report[19]

This quarterly publication attempts to give the latest estimates for population, births, mortality rate, and infant mortality rate. The date corresponding to each statistic is given along side. For example, the issue of the *Population and Vital Statistics Report* dated Oct., 1984 has some figures for 1983; others from 1981; others from 1971; etc.

12. International Historical Statistics: Africa and Asia[20]

Most of this publication covers economic statistics. The vital statistics are births, deaths, and infant mortality. The years covered vary, but are generally 1900-1949.

Statistics—Sources—By Country

The compilations of statistics cited previously are convenient. However, the information given is usually very brief. In addition, the information given often is derived from publications of the individual countries. This section gives some of the source publications from the originating countries.

Many countries issue their own statistical abstracts or statistical yearbooks. These may be obtained directly from those countries. Also, the Congressional Information Service (CIS) reproduces and issues some of these in a series called *Current National Statistical Compendiums*.[21] They are made available in microfiche. An example is *Kenya. Central Bureau of Statistics. Statistical abstract 1980*. The whole range of statistics is presented in these abstracts, including data on health. There are, in addition, statistical abstracts/ yearbooks for regions of the world, e.g., *Statistical Yearbook for Asia and the Pacific*.[22]

It may be convenient to access the statistical information via computer. For example, the U.S. Bureau of the Census has magnetic tapes on domestic data available for purchase. The Bureau of the Census also has an *International Data Base* with statistics on 203 countries. Data are derived from the host countries' publications. Currently, only federal agencies and the contractors of federal agencies may use the data base. Originally, it would have been possible for others to purchase the magnetic tapes for use on their own computers, but federal budget cuts have gotten in the way. Now, the only way to get the data is to order the tables in paper copy. There are 94 tables of information covering such topics as health and nutrition, mortality, migration, family planning, and literacy. Not all the tables have data from all the countries. For example, Table 22 is "Daily per capita protein supply," with about 10 countries included. Table 23 is "Percent Malnourished." Significantly, there are no

Articles in the *American Journal of Tropical Medicine and Hygiene* have been cited these journals:

> *Transactions of the Royal Society of Tropical Medicine and Hygiene*
> *Journal of Parasitology*
> *Journal of Immunology*
> *Bulletin of the World Health Organization*
> *Experimental Parasitology*

For the social sciences, there is the counterpart volume, *SSCI journal citation reports*.

Popular Press

During a famine, there is a lot in the popular press. The *NY Times Index* and *Readers Guide to Periodical Literature* will probably be adequate to finding this information.

ORGANIZATIONS

The following are some organizations that regularly gather statistics on Third World countries and issue reports with those statistics.

1. United Nations. New York, NY 10017.
2. World Health Organization. Geneva, Switzerland. Regional Office for the Americas. Washington, DC 20037.
3. Food and Agricultural Organization. Rome, Italy. Liaison Office for North America. Washington, DC 20437.
4. World Bank or International Bank for Reconstruction and Development. Washington, DC 20433.
5. U.S. Census. Bureau of the Census. Dept of Commerce. Washington, DC 20233.
6. Agency for International Development. Washington, DC 20523.

CONCLUSION

Getting the facts is difficult because of a lack of critical compilation. M. Morris states: "There are no numbers tucked away in the

Sahel, Paris, or New York that—subjected to some process of imaginative compilation—could tell people what they need to know about the individual Sahelian states or the region."[40] It may not be the role of the librarian to judge the usefulness of the information available. However, supplying the numbers to the patron may not be enough. Giving the available statistics and also the information on possible shortcomings would be a more valuable service. The tragedy that is occurring in Africa and elsewhere requires the vigorous dissemination of the best information available.

REFERENCES

1. United Nations. Department of International Economic and Social Affairs. *Report on the world social situation.* New York: United Nations; 1982: p. 64.
2. Garcia, Rolando V.; Escudero, Jose C. *The constant catastrophe: malnutrition, famines and drought* (Drought and man, the 1972 case history, v.2). New York: Pergamon Press; 1982: p. 195.
3. United Nations. Department of International Economic and Social Affairs. Statistical Office. *Demographic Yearbook.* New York: United Nations; 1984.
4. Ibid. p. 33.
5. Ibid. p. 18.
6. Morris, Morris D. *Measuring the condition of the world's poor: the physical quality of life index.* New York: Pergamon Press; 1979.
7. Morris, Morris D.; Brandel, Sarah K. *Appropriate indicators of social progress in the Sahel.* (Overseas Development Council, Working paper no. 6). Washington: Overseas Development Council; 1982, p. viii.
8. United Nations. Department of International Economic and Social Affairs. Statistical Office. *Statistical Yearbook.* New York: United Nations; 1983.
9. World Health Organization. *World Health Statistics Annual.* Geneva: World Health Organization; 1984.
10. World Bank. *World Development Report.* New York: Oxford University Press; 1984.
11. World Bank. *World tables: v. II. Social data from the data files of the World Bank.* 3rd ed. Baltimore: Johns Hopkins University Press; 1984.
12. Ibid. p. ix.
13. Kurian, George Thomas. *Encyclopedia of the Third World.* Revised ed. New York: Facts on File; 1982.
14. Ibid. p. xiii.
15. *World population.* Washington: U.S. Department of Commerce, Bureau of the Census; 1973- .
16. Food and Agriculture Organization of the United Nations. *FAO Production Yearbook.* Rome: Food and Agriculture Organization; 1984.
17. *World Factbook.* Washington: Central Intelligence Agency; 1981- .
18. World Bank. *World Bank atlas.* Washington: World Bank; 1983.
19. United Nations. Department of International Economic and Social Affairs. Statistical Office. *Population and Vital Statistics Report.* New York: United Nations; 1949- .
20. Mitchell, B. R. *International historical statistics: Asia and Africa.* New York: New York University Press; 1982.
21. *Current National Statistical Compendiums.* Washington: Congressional Information Service; 1970-

22. *Statistical Yearbook for Asia and the Pacific.* Bangkok, Thailand: Economic and Social Commission for Asia and the Pacific; 1981.

23. Goyer, Doreen S.; Domschke, Eliane. *Handbook of national population censuses: Latin America and the Caribbean, North America, and Oceania.* Westport, CT: Greenwood Press; 1983.

24. Kpedekpo, G. M. K.; Arya, P. L. *Social and economic statistics for Africa.* London: George Allen & Unwin; 1981.

25. Wasserman, Paul et al., eds. *Statistics sources: a subject guide to data on industrial, business, social, educational, financial, and other topics for the United States and internationally.* 9th ed. Detroit: Gale Research Co.; 1984. 2v.

26. *Index to International Statistics.* Washington: Congressional Information Service; 1983- .

27. *American Statistics Index.* Washington: Congressional Information Service; 1973- .

28. Mata, Leonardo J. *The children of Santa Maria Cauque: a prospective field study of health and growth.* Cambridge, MA: MIT Press, 1978.

29. Jelliffe, E. F. P. *Protein-calorie malnutrition of early childhood: two decades of malnutrition, a bibliography.* Farnham Royal, Slough: Commonwealth Agricultural Bureaux; 1975.

30. Ghosh, Pradip K., ed. *Health, food, and nutrition in Third World development.* Westport, CT: Greenwood Press; 1984.

31. Chen, Lincoln C.; Scrimshaw, Nevin S., eds. *Diarrhea and malnutrition: interactions, mechanisms, and interventions.* New York: Plenum Press; 1983: p.3.

32. Warren, Kenneth S.; Hoffman, Donald B. *Schistosomiasis III: abstracts of the complete literature 1963-1974.* Washington: Hemisphere Publ. Corp.; 1976. 2v.

33. Warren, Kenneth S.; Newill, Vaun A. *Schistosomiasis: a bibliography of the world's literature from 1852 to 1962.* Cleveland: The Press of Western Reserve University; 1967. 2v.

34. Warren, Kenneth S. *Schistosomiasis: the evolution of a medical literature, selected abstracts and citations, 1852-1972.* Cambridge, MA: MIT Press; 1973.

35. Saunders, Robert J.; Warford, Jeremy J. *Village water supply: economics and policy in the developing world.* Baltimore: Johns Hopkins University Press; 1976.

36. United Nations. *World population trends and prospects by country, 1950-2000: summary report of the 1978 assessment.* New York: United Nations; 1979.

37. United Nations. Department of International Economic and Social Affairs. *Levels and trends of mortality since 1950: a joint study by the United Nations and the World Health Organization.* New York: United Nations; 1982.

38. Caldwell, John C., ed. *The persistence of high fertility: population prospects in the Third World.* Canberra: Department of Demography, A. N. U.; 1977. 2v.

39. Garfield, Eugene, ed. *SCI Journal Citation Reports, a Bibliometric Analysis of Science Journals in the ISI Data Base.* Philadelphia: Institute for Scientific Information; 1984.

40. Morris. *Appropriate.* p. 81.

	DROUGHT	FAMINE	MALNUTRITION	STARVATION
DATABASES				
A400	159	48	56	116
BIOB	1202	80	25991	3373
BIOL	2568	54	41924	5933
CAIN	2584	250	2908	1077
COMP	238	9	7	179
DISS	365	77	183	389
ECER	1	4	109	12
EMED	60	24	2706	1901
ERIC	30	46	255	41
GPOM	60	9	22	7
HLTH	19	32	604	110
INFO	189	50	41	94
INSB	43	2	1	29
INSP	205	8	6	95
IPAB	0	0	91	28
MESH	50	33	3107	2941
MS78	32	47	1677	1814
MS74	12	20	939	1235
MS70	8	10	520	1085
MGMT	109	39	19	32
NTIS	638	18	229	225
PAIS	133	42	65	15
POLL	103	1	9	64
PSYC	8	13	392	239
PTSL	1094	63	85	146
PTSP	780	36	69	131
RELI	21	60	10	28
SOCA	36	85	87	53
SSCB	37	91	127	34
SSCI	141	230	323	128

Figure 2. BRS CROS Search. March, 1985.
The searches were the following:
  Drought or Droughts
  Famine or Famines
  Malnourish$ or Malnutrition
  (The "$" is the truncation symbol in BRS)
  Starv$

controlled indexing vocabulary would usually be in order. These postings may be looked upon as rough indicators; some include many false drops. For example, "drought" in INFO or MGMT may be a business drought. "Famine" does not have that many contexts, but "malnutrition" does. Use the comparative advantages of the data bases. BIOL may have a lot of citations on droughts but SSCI may be better if you want more of a social orientation.

Other search systems have data bases that would also be useful.

Nutrition Abstracts and Reviews is part of the CAB Abstracts file on DIALOG. POPLINE is a file on the National Library of Medicine MEDLARS system. This latter data base focuses on fertility and population planning in the Third World. It also has good coverage on other important Third World health problems.

There are other indexes/abstracts which are important for this subject that are not now available for computerized searching. *Population Index* is one of these. Another index/abstract that is not online now is the *Quarterly Bibliography of Major Tropical Diseases.* This publication is sponsored by the UNDP/World Bank/WHO Special Programme for Research and Training in Tropical Diseases and is produced by NLM. The preface states that its purpose is to stimulate research within the Third World countries themselves. It is a very handy source for the six tropical diseases covered (list in part III). To illustrate, look up "Leishmaniasis" in *Index Medicus.* There are several subheadings such as diagnosis, drug therapy, and occurrence. In *QBMTD,* there are all the subheadings found in *IM* plus other terms positioned as subheadings that help specify the area needed under the disease heading. For example, under Leishmaniasis some headings are insect vectors, lymphocytes, and travel. Many of the citations contain abstracts. The abstracts can be found in the Author Section.

Journals

As usual, the key to the journal literature is through the indexes and abstracts. To find the main journals in these fields, check the annual volume of the *SCI journal citation reports.*[39] As an example, for the biomedical part, one might start with a prominent periodical like the *American Journal of Tropical Medicine and Hygiene* and see its cited and citing pattern. Articles in the *American Journal of Tropical Medicine and Hygiene* have been cited most by these journals:

> *Transactions of the Royal Society of Tropical Medicine and Hygiene*
> *Experimental Parasitology*
> *Mosquito News*
> *Advances in Virus Research*
> *Journal of Medical Entomology*
> *Journal of Immunology*

NEW REFERENCE WORKS IN SCIENCE AND TECHNOLOGY

Robert G. Krupp, Editor

Reviewers for this column are: Carmela Carbone (CC), Engineering Societies Library, New York, NY; Kerry Kresse (KLK), University of Kentucky, Lexington, KY; Robert G. Krupp (RGK), Maplewood, NJ; Barbara A. List (BAL), Columbia University, New York, NY; Ellis Mount (EM), Columbia University, New York, NY; and David A. Tyckoson (DAT), Iowa State University, Ames, IA.

EARTH SCIENCES

Energy products specifications guide: conservation, solar, wind, and photovoltaics. Harrisville, NH: SolarVision, Inc.; 1984. 757p. $49.50. No ISBN provided.

 This book is a compilation of descriptions and specifications for products currently on the market in the solar energy field. All types of equipment are covered, including solar components and subsystems for buildings, complete solar energy systems for buildings, high-efficiency building products, power generation equipment, monitoring and data collection devices, and computer software and services. For each product the physical specifications, performance test data, installation and maintenance requirements, guarantee/warranty, and pricing information are provided. Photographs, diagrams, and graphs of performance accompany many of the entries. All of the information is provided by the manufacturers and users of each product and the results are examined by the editors of *Solar*

Age magazine. If they feel that the information provided is incorrect, the device is independently tested for verification. With the rapid changes in the solar energy industry, this guide will be updated annually. Over 1,000 products are contained in the directory, and this book should be consulted by anyone purchasing solar equipment. (DAT)

Field guide to soils and the environment applications of soil surveys. By Gerald W. Olson. New York: Chapman and Hall; 1984. 219p. $18.95. ISBN 0-412-25970-2 (pbk).

This guide can provide teachers and learners with exercises that will lead to confidence in the manipulation and utilization of soil survey data. Emphasis is given initiative and imagination in the applications of soil surveys. Very well illustrated. Others who should be interested in this work include agronomists, conservationists, ecologists, and soil scientists. (RGK).

Mineral resources: a world review. By John A. Wolfe. New York: Chapman and Hall; 1984. 293p. $18.95(paper). ISBN 0-412-25190-6.

This reference tool is designed for those interested in the mineral sources and economy related to them but with training in another field. Part I is a series of short essays on various aspects of the mineral industries (such as history, mineral policies of various countries, economics, exploration, and even crystal gazing). Part II, as a condensed review of the most important mineral commodities, is the reference backbone of this work. Included in this section are reports on 21 metals and 18 non-metals, 43 figures and seven tables. There is an annotated bibliography which unfortunately is rather lean. The glossary is well-prepared and useful. This overview individual countries included. The data that the U.N. puts out is somewhat constrained by the political sensitivity of the host countries. The individual countries do not, however, have a voice in what the U.S. Census publishes.

One problem with finding statistical information is that many countries have never conducted a census. To find census information, the *Handbook of national population censuses: Latin America and the Caribbean, North America, and Oceania*[23] may be helpful. Subsequent volumes will cover Asia, Africa, and Europe. For Africa, there is a publication, *Social and economic statistics for Africa.*[24] See, in particular, chapter 3, "Health Statistics."

Statistics—Sources—Indexes

Statistics Sources[25]

This is a very convenient entry point for specific statistics. *Statistics sources* is an index to information contained in prominent sources, e.g., *Demographic Yearbook,* and to some lesser known ones. For example, one may be interested in finding the number of doctors in Indonesia. There is an entry: "Indonesia-Health-Number of Physicians." This entry leads to the *Statistical Yearbook* and to the particular section, "Health-Hospital Establishments and Health Personnel" on p. 318.

Index to International Statistics[26]

This publication indexes statistics from documents issued by several agencies. Many of the documents are from the United Nations and OECD (Organization For Economic Cooperation and Development). There are several useful entry points:

— a large subject index;
— an index by category which includes: age, commodity, country, individual company, industry, sex;
— an index by issuing source;
— an index by title.

American Statistics Index[27]

The format is the same as that of the *Index to International Statistics.* Both are produced by the Congressional Information Service. *ASI* concentrates on statistics derived from U.S. government publications, though the subjects covered include conditions in other countries.

Statistics—Longitudinal Studies

Because the data collected by Third World countries is often inadequate, it may be beneficial to also examine individual case studies that have several years of statistics included. One such study is reported in the book, *The children of Santa Maria Cauque: a prospective field study of health and growth.*[28]

FAMINE'S ONGOING COROLLARY: SELECTED DISEASES OF THE THIRD WORLD

Although the statistics are necessary to analyze the problems and develop possible remedies, a look at some of the conditions caused by malnutrition is in order. Listed here are first, conditions directly caused by malnutrition, and second, diseases of the Third World that are prevalent and worsened by malnutrition. Check the bibliography for literature on them.

Diseases directly related to malnutrition

A. Kwashiorkor[29,30] is caused by the lack of protein in the diet. It is most prevalent in children ages 1-3 and the physical signs include edema.
B. Marasmus[29,30] is also usually a condition of protein deficiency. With this disease, however, the children are very thin and appear to be wasting away.
C. Xerophthalmia is caused by a vitamin A deficiency and may result in blindness.

Other selected diseases of the Third World

A. Diarrheal Diseases. As an indication of the role that malnutrition plays in the health of Third World populations, Chen/Scrimshaw state: "In Latin America, for example, diarrhea was found to be by far the major infectious cause of death in children below age 5, and malnutrition was noted to be a direct or underlying cause of most deaths."[31]

B. Schistosomiasis is a parasitic disease that is widespread in tropical areas and infects several organs, including the liver, spleen, and bladder. It is one disease that is very well indexed.[32,33,34]

C. The *Quarterly Bibliography of Major Tropical Diseases (QBMTD)* covers filariasis, leishmaniasis, leprosy, malaria, schistosomiasis, and trypanosomiasis. It includes diseases that may not pose large health problems in the Developed Countries, but are significant in the Third World.

Prominent non-nutritional factors in disease

Clean Water. It would be a large oversight not to mention the part water plays. The use of contaminated water is a major factor in the spread of the many infectious diseases cited above.[35]

Population. Since World War II, the mortality rate in the Third World has come down dramatically, although it still is very large in comparison to the Developed Countries. The very high birth rate in those poorer countries has come down very little in comparison. These countries are therefore experiencing large population increases when their economies and health care systems are not able to support this growth.[36,37,38]

THE LITERATURE

Because the problems of drought, famine, and malnutrition have so many aspects to them, many disciplines would contribute relevant information. The journal literature, especially in the sciences, will be important. However, technical reports/government documents and regular monographs will need to be consulted as well. Several monographs are cited in the References at the end of this paper. For technical reports, check the publications issued by the organizations listed in section V.

Indexes/Abstracts

To give an indication of which indexes/abstracts may be useful, see Figure 2. This is a tabulation of citations from the Bibliographic Retrieval Services (BRS) CROS data base. Postings were drawn via a simple, free text search. Since there would be many synonyms to consider and subjects to combine in an actual search, the use of a should be available on the reference shelves in most physical science and earth science libraries in academe, industry, and government. The author and compiler is a consulting geologist and is with Taysan Copper, Inc. (RGK)

ENGINEERING TECHNOLOGY

(The) Acid rain sourcebook. Edited by Thomas C. Elliott and Robert G. Schwieger. New York: McGraw-Hill; 1984. 290 p. $37.50. ISBN 0-07-606540-5.

A reference collection of specialized information discussions on areas critical to the acid rain issue: problem definition, impact of legislation, emissions standards, international perspective, cost scenarios, and engineering solutions. The text is reinforced with 130 illustrations and about 50 tables. Literature cited is very current. For industrial, academic, and public libraries concerned technically and emotionally about acid rain. (RGK)

Aerospace dictionary: English-French-German-Spanish. Montreuil: Gauthier-Villars; 1984. 828p. $85.00. ISBN 2-04-011952-3.

This quadrilingual dictionary's 36,000 entries are *only* in English. Access to the source entries in the other languages is covered in three other volumes. Indication of applications is given for each with the use of 45 categories (e.g., manufacturing, testing, equipment, engineering). For special library collections in aerospace industries and in larger universities. (RGK)

American university programs in computer science. Edited by William W. Lau. Fullerton, CA: GGL Educational Press; 1984. 210 p. $18.00. ISBN 0-915751-25-9.

> Choosing a college or university is often a difficult task, but one that this book hopes to make easier for the student contemplating studies in computer science. It lists 160 colleges and universities in the United States with programs in computer science. For each institution, a brief description is provided of both the overall university environment and the computer science (or equivalent) department and computing facilities. One unique aspect of this guide is that it provides a course listing of every computer science class offered at each university covered on both the graduate and undergraduate levels. An unfortunate omission is that, at least for my institution, the computer science department is listed but the computer engineering department is not. Depite this specific lack the tabulation will be valuable to high school students selecting a college or to students considering transferring from one institution to another. (DAT)

Building better beds. By Percy W. Blandford. Blue Ridge Summit, PA: TAB; 1984. 308p. $19.95. ISBN 0-8306-0664-5.

> This is a rare book on a very common subject. Coverage is exclusively on beds, including cribs and many specialty varieties (e.g., folding). Extensive illustrative matter and very detailed instructions, mostly obviously of the carpentry aspects, thus brass beds are omitted. For personal purchase and public libraries. (RGK)

Building bridges: history, technology, construction. By Hans Wittfoht. Düsseldorf: Beton-Verlag; 1984. 327p. $99.00. ISBN 3-7640-0176-3. (Distributed by Heyden.)

>This reference work is of rare quality, style, and beauty, all combined with a level of professionalism and scholarship which makes it ideal not only for the most technical collections but also for a large readership who are not only nonspecialists but just plain bridge lovers. The large bridges, especially those with daring structure systems, are virtually flaunted in a most delightful manner with coverage being indeed worldwide. Let not the purchase price (high but not unbelievable) daunt those eager to acquire a work of this caliber. Some 500 striking black and white photographs are included but the accompanying text is also not to be ignored as it constitutes painless instructions (sans calculations) on bridge building from way back and on into the future. The author and compiler is a renowned bridge builder. The work is a translated and revised edition of *Triumph der Spannweiten.* (RGK)

Chance Vought F-4U Corsair. 2d ed. By Edward T. Maloney and Thomas E. Doll. Fallbrook, CA: Aero Publishers; 1984. 68p. $6.95. ISBN 0-8168-0541-5. (Aero series Vol. 11.)

>Primarily a photo history of the use of the Vought F4U Corsair airplane from its 1938 design until after World War II and the Korean War in 1952. Some 250 mostly black and white photographs are provided. A reference work for collections on the history of aeronautics. (RGK)

(The) Computer and telecommunications handbook. By Jeff Maynard. London: Granada; 1984. 237p. $25.00. ISBN 0-246-12253-6. (Distributed by Sheridan House, Dobbs Ferry, NY.)

> A well-organized collection of miscellaneous information useful to the computer and the telecommunication practitioner, hence important to research and technology collections in industry concerned with telecommunications. Excellent index. Author's affiliation not given. (RGK)

Computers and information processing world index. Edited by Suzan Deigton and others. Phoenix, AZ: Oryx; 1984. 616p. $85.00. ISBN 0-89774-116-1.

> A rather ambitious but at times somewhat confusing attempt to provide a *World index* designed as a guide to the literature of "computing." Four obvious sections are used involving 715 international organizations, 396 reference works and literature guides, 1012 computing applications publications, and 825 journal titles. Included too is a useful compilation of 19 "standardizing bodies." There is also an extensive collection of publishers' addresses, much of which is duplicative of data given in the body of the work. The index is referred to as "simple" but because no explanatory section is provided, its rationale and hence its value is a bit depreciated. As with any major directory of this type, currency is important and is indeed touted but in fact non-current data are peppered throughout (e.g., Bell Labs operations should be called AT&T-Bell Laboratories). Inconsistencies are common (e.g., number groupings for American telephone numbers vary: 703/321 4900; 202 357 9629; (415) 3266200; or, no attempt at standardization of "notes" about the libraries themselves). Nevertheless, despite this scattering of shortcomings, the work should be seriously considered for any collection on computer sciences and services. (RGK)

Concrete admixtures handbook; properties, science, and technology. Edited by V. S. Ramachandran. Park Ridge, NJ: Noyes Publications; 1984. 626p. $72.00. ISBN 0-8155-0981-2.

Admixtures are ingredients that are added to the concrete batch immediately before or during mixing to confer certain beneficial properties to concrete. This handbook deals with the science, properties, specifications, dispensing, availability, limitations, patents, and other aspects of the commonly used admixtures. The book is divided into 10 chapters and all the important admixtures are included. Each chapter contains a list of important recent references as a guide for further reading. A chapter on cement science is included to describe the most recent concepts so that the subsequent chapters can easily be followed. The last chapter on patents describes how a variety of materials can be used as admixtures for various effects. (CC)

Construction materials ready-reference manual. By Joseph J. Waddell. McGraw-Hill; 1985. 395p. $24.50. ISBN 0-07-067649-6.

This is a handy field manual providing basic information on the principal materials of construction. Each chapter covers one major building material (e.g., concrete, plastics). It is not meant to replace standard reference volumes but serve as a quickly and conveniently available tool at a construction site. The author is a consulting engineer. (RGK)

Data systems dictionary: German-English; English-German. 2d ed. By Karl-Heinz Brinkmann and Rudolf Schmidt. Wiesbaden: Oscar Brandstetter; 1979. 334p. $41.00 (paper). ISBN 3-87097-095-2.

A 1979 edition, with close to 30,000 terms in *each* of the two sections (German-English; English-German). Still, a good tool for translators needing some historical perspective and for collections with strength in data systems. (RGK)

Dictionary of electrical engineering, telecommunications and electronics. Volume III (English-German-French). Compiled by W. Goedecke. Wiesbaden: Brandstetter Verlag; 1967 (1974 reprint). 1252p. $43.00. ISBN 3-87097-015-4.

This is third (and final) part of a trilingual dictionary of some 30,000 engineering and communication terms in English, German, and French, with English as the key language in this part. Note, though, that this is a 1974 reprint of a 1967 work and while up-to-date at the time of original publication, it may now not cover phraseology which has emerged in recent years. However, its comprehensiveness may serve translators well if the volume supplements a collection of more recent works. (RGK)

Dictionary of metallurgy and foundry technology, English-German. Edited by Karl Stölzel. Amsterdam: Elsevier Science Publishers; 1984. 418p. $69.25 ISBN 0-444-99612-5.

The aim of this work is to provide a relatively extensive (one-way: English to German) dictionary containing both highly specialized, exclusively metallurgical terms and a great number of definitions also encountered in related fields. For certain terms, keyword explanations have been included for the non-specialist. The dictionary contains about 37,000 entries. Topics covered include ore dressing and auxiliary materials, pig-iron and steel production, powder metallurgy, non-ferrous metallurgy and metal-forming processes. Many terms involving hardening, surface treatment, and corrosion are also included. (CC)

Dictionary of naval abbreviations. Compiled and edited by Bill Wedertz. Annapolis, MD: Naval Institute Press; 1984. 3d ed. 330p. $15.95. ISBN 0-87021-155-2.

This edition of the *Dictionary of naval abbreviations* (DIC-NAVAB) contains an updated list of over 15,000 abbreviations used in naval communications. For each abbreviation, a listing of all possible words or phrases matching that abbreviation is provided. Entries range from the simple (FCC, Fleet Command Center) to the complex (FLECOMBDIRSYSTRACEN-PAC, Fleet Combat Direction Systems Training Center, Pacific). All of the terms are currently in use; the World War II era terms included in the first two editions have been removed. Even with this effort to limit the size of the work, the compilation is a monument to military bureaucracy and the author's attempts to organize it. This work is essential in understanding naval communications and should be included in any library with a collection in military and naval science. (DAT)

Dictionary of nuclear engineering in four languages: English, German, French, Russian. Compiled by Ralf Sube. New York: Elsevier 1985. 1199p. $144.25. ISBN 0-444-99593-5.

For this dictionary nuclear engineering has been defined in its general sense as applied nuclear physics, i.e., industrial and other applications of nuclear power, isotopes and ionizing radiation, together with their scientific and technological fundamentals. Its main point of emphasis is the nuclear fuel cycle. Also included are other applications of nuclear power inclusive of the military sector, nuclear fusion, and methods and equipment encountered in isotope and radiation technology. The entire biological aspect has been excluded, however. In the compilation of terms, great attention was given only to generally valid basic expressions and to special terms where these occurred in all four languages. (CC)

Effective lighting for home and business. By Dan Ramsey. Blue Ridge Summit, PA: TAB; 1984. 213p. $18.95. ISBN 0-8306-0658-0.

>Describes in simple language how lighting works, choice of appropriate lighting, and how to install, maintain, and repair lights, wires, switches, and fixtures. Considerable illustrative matter. As the author says, the work offers "new light on an illuminating subject." For personal purchase and public libraries. (RGK)

Electroplating engineering handbook. 4th ed. Edited by Lawrence J. Durney. New York: Van Nostrand; 1984. 790p. $69.50. ISBN 0-442-22002-2.

>Revisions of the 3d edition (13 years old) involved 44 chapters (or sub-chapters) and resulted in a new handbook, somewhat more compact, but covering rather completely new technologies in the metal finishing industry. The index is excellent. However, a random check of 19 chapters and sub-chapters involving 600 references revealed that only about 30% were dated after 1971 and 12 chapters involved no citations after 1971. For most physical science collections in industry and academe. (RGK)

Focke-Wulf 190. 2d ed. By Eberhard Weber. Fallbrook, CA: Aero Publishers; 1984. 64p. $3.95. ISBN 0-8168-0569-5. (Aero series Vol. 18.)

>A gallery of mostly black and white photos (about 150) of this aircraft's development from design in 1938 to demise in 1944. An excellent reference tool for collections on the history of aeronautics. (RGK)

Fluid power design handbook. By Frank Yeaple. New York: Dekker; 1984. 614p. $83.50. ISBN 0-8247-7196-6.

> Step-by-step techniques in this book show how to incorporate all types of hydraulic and pneumatic components into systems, to control them, and predict performance. Included are critical analyses of items such as pumps, compressors, valves, and a dozen others. Details are given for practical tests (e.g., for fatigue). Positive design procedures are established. For collections strong in fluid power technology and hydraulic machinery. Author is with *Design News.* (RGK)

44 terrific woodworking plans and projects. By Raymond D. Brown. Blue Ridge Summit, PA: TAB; 1984. 234p. $21.95. ISBN 0-8306-0762-5.

> This collection of plans is for the use of amateur woodworkers. Instructions on how to read them and build from them are included. Heavily and excellently illustrated. A manual for personal purchase and for the public library. (RGK)

Handbook of concrete engineering. 2d ed. Edited by Mark Fintel. New York: Van Nostrand Reinhold; 1985. 892p. $89.50. ISBN 0-442-22623-3.

> This handbook contains up-to-date information on planning, design, analysis, and construction of engineered concrete structures. Its intention is to provide engineers, architects, contractors, and students of civil engineering and architecture with authoritative practical design information. Since the publication of the first edition of the handbook in 1974, there have been many innovations in design techniques, particularly as a result of the wide use of computers in design offices. The American Concrete Institute code that serves as the basis for concrete design has undergone two revisions; this edition of the handbook is based on the 1983 version of the ACI code. Reflected in this edition are the great progress in construction equipment and methods and the availability of higher strength

materials. There are new chapters on post-tensioned slab systems, parking structures, and structural plain concrete. All other chapters have been thoroughly revised to incorporate the changes brought about by the 1977 and 1983 ACI codes. (CC).

Handbook of data sheets for solution of mechanical systems problems. By Robert W. Roose and Thomas R. Roose. New York: Van Nostrand; 1984. 407p. $48.50. ISBN 0-442-27804-7.

This compilation of 195 data sheets has been selected from articles published over the past 30 years, mostly in *Heating/Piping/Air Conditioning.* Many of the sheets are nomographs. Five general categories divide the applications: general, basic heat transfer, heating, air conditioning and ventilation, and industrial and process piping. For mechanical engineers and contractors working with large buildings and industrial plants. The subject index is a bit on the lean side. (RGK)

Handbook of metal forming. Edited by Kurt Lange. New York: McGraw-Hill; 1985. Mixed pagination. $85.00. ISBN 0-07-036285-8.

The contents of this translated handbook are based mainly on the German *Lehrbuch der Umformtechnik* which was published in three volumes from 1972 to 1975. In this English edition, the material has been updated and expanded. This includes the introduction of recent developments in processes, materials, tools, and equipment, as well as the adaptation to U.S. terminology, standards, and units. The book is intended to be a broad general introduction to the fundamentals of metal-forming technology, tribology, technical theory of plasticity, materials properties, and process data determination. Also dealt with are production methods, tools, machine tools, and other equipment as well as tool-manufacturing methods and problems of production economy. Among the useful appendices are tables of comparative designations of steels and of non-ferrous metals and chemical compositions of steels and of non-ferrous metals. (CC)

Handbook of oil industry terms and phrases. 4th ed. By R. D. Langenkamp. Tulsa, OK: PennWell Books; 1984. 347p. $25.00. ISBN 0-87814-258-4.

> The scope of this fourth edition has been broadened to include hundreds of geological terms. The definitions and explanations of the geological subjets will aid the non-geologist and the non-oil person to understand the nature and occurrence of minerals and rocks in the earth and the underground structures and formations that are petroleum's realm. Also included are entries on new equipment, advances in drilling technology and operating methods, investment funds, operating interests, royalty interests, and nondrilling leases. (CC)

Home remodelling—a how-to money-saving handbook. By Betty Galeman Wahlfeldt. Blue Ridge Summit, PA: TAB; 1984. 388p. $24.95. ISBN 0-8306-0215-1.

> A well-illustrated how-to-do-it book for the home remodeler. Designed for use by the younger generation who may wish to rehabilitate older homes, not for aesthetic reasons so much, but to save money. Step-by-step procedures provide instruction not easily found in most literature on the subject. Best for personal purchase and public libraries. (RGK)

Manufacturing cost engineering handbook. Edited by Eric M. Malstrom. New York: Marcel Dekker; 1984. 447p. $59.75. ISBN 0-8247-7126-5.

> Cost engineering is a field that involves the application of scientific principles to the problems of cost estimation, cost control, and profitability. With the current state of the economy, cost engineering is essential to the survival of any engineering project. This handbook covers all aspects of the cost engineering discipline, including cost estimating, cost control, computer methods, engineering economics, and analysis tools. Each chapter is written by an expert in the field and includes numerous charts, tables, and formulae that can be used by the practicing engineer. For each type of problem en-

countered on a project there are a number of clear examples showing how it may be solved. This work may be used both as a textbook for courses on cost engineering and as a sourcebook for professional engineers. (DAT)

Master handbook of electronic tables and formulas. 4th ed. By Martin Clifford. Blue Ridge Summit, PA: TAB; 1984. 382p. $21.95. ISBN 0-8306-0625-4.

Represents a way of solving electronics problems by arranging electronics data in tabular form. Time and work are thus saved. An excellent companion at work or study and best for personal purchase. (RGK)

Micro software for business. By InfoSource, Inc. Radnor, PA: Chilton; 1984. Mixed pagination. $19.95(paper). ISBN 0-8019-7430-5(pbk).

Provides 2771 business packages, organized by application, and indexed by product, vendor, and machine/operating system. The directory is primarily for those who are evaluating and using business software packages. The software profiles are designed to tell if the product being described meets the consumer's requirements without being verbose. For business and industrial libraries. (RGK)

NBS/NRC steam tables: Thermodynamic and transport properties and computer programs for vapor and liquid states of water in SI units. Compiled by Lester Haar and others. New York: Hemisphere; 1984. 320p. $34.50. ISBN 0-89116-354-9.

>Contains tables of thermodynamic property values based on a formulation made possible by correlation of the large body of thermodynamic measurements for water and steam. Included too are tables of transport and other physical property values. The data are presented in eleven detailed tables (with the one on compressed water and superheated steam being the most extensive—such as the Helmholtz Function, computer programs, and equations for transport. Seventy percent of the 70-item set of references are dated pre-1980. For engineering collections in industry and academe. (RGK)

Oil economists' handbook 1985. By Gilbert Jenkins. London: Elsevier Applied Science Publishers; 1985. 378p. $90.00. ISBN 0-85334-325-X.

>The purpose of this book is to provide a ready reference for those working both inside and outside the oil and energy industries. A dictionary section is concerned with the jargon, abbreviations, and terms used in the oil industry. In addition to the numerous statistical entries in the dictionary, the data section is composed of energy and oil statistics and data useful to oil economists. Much of the value of the book will be found in the historical statistics. There is international coverage of energy resources, energy production, transportation, petroleum refining, petroleum products, storage, energy economics, pricing, and energy companies. There are 180 tables in all. Finally, there is a chronology section composed of events which have had significant impact in the international energy field. (CC)

Power capacitor handbook. By T. Longland and others. London: Butterworths; 1984. 308p. $59.95. ISBN 0-408-00292-1.

> A reference tool not only for the electrical engineer in industry who has some vested interest in the output efficiency of his electrical system, but for financial management at high levels. Thus the concern over the use of power-factor capacitors to gain a more economical use of electrical power. The authors spell out in great detail the equipment and methodologies involved in improving the power-factor. Literature references cited are rather scant but well-chosen. (RGK)

Professional plumbing techniques—illustrated and simplified. By Arthur J. Smith. Blue Ridge Summit, PA: TAB; 1984. 281p. $15.95. ISBN 0-8306-0763-3.

> An alphabetical arrangement of 158 topics relating to techniques used by professional plumbers. Much illustrative matter. No subject index. For public libraries and personal purchase. (RGK)

Quality technology handbook. 4th ed. Compiled and edited by R. S. Sharpe and others. London: Butterworths; 1984. 485p. $85.00. ISBN 0-408-01331-1. (ISSN 0266-3104.)

> This is really a combination handbook and directory, the bulk of which (920 entries) comprise the latter category. These entries are grouped by country (409 countries are covered). Earlier sections provide a plethora of data on non-destructive testing, mostly of a non-technical nature but involving areas such as quality assurance, literature, and standards. For strong engineering collections, especially where data about the United Kingdom is essential. (RGK)

(The) TAB handbook of hand & power tools. By Rudolf F. Graf and George J. Whalen. Blue Ridge Summit, PA: TAB; 1984. 501p. $26.95. ISBN 0-8306-0638-6.

> Provides descriptions of a great number and variety of tools, especially for home use. Note that projects, as such, are *not* described. Tools are shown in use of minor facets on larger projects. Hence the emphasis is on *use* rather than how to make an item or do a repair. For the most part power tools are covered in Part 2. Happily, throughout the work high attention is given safety. Considerable illustrative matter. For personal purchase and public libraries. (RGK)

Wörterbuch technischer begriffe mit 4300 definitionen nach DIN. Deutsch und English. 3d ed. Compiled by Henry G. Freeman. Berlin: Beuth; 1983. 703p. $87.00 (paper). ISBN 3-410-11594-3. (Distributed by Heyden.)

> The 4300 definitions in this essentially German language dictionary provide a rich working tool for those interested in international communication and technology (as given by DIN). The English translation immediately follows the German text but there is happily also an English to German vocabulary list for the keywords in the main body. (RGK)

LIFE SCIENCES

Arkansas ferns and fern allies. By W. Carl Taylor, illustrated by Paul W. Nelson. Milwaukee: Milwaukee Public Museum; 1984. 262p. $32.00. ISBN 0-89326-097-5.

> Ferns are some of nature's most graceful plants, and Arkansas is fortunate to have so many. Taylor's handbook is an excellent guide to Arkansas ferns, aimed toward the botanist and experienced amateur. The descriptions of each species are clear and concise, and are illustrated. Nelson's black and white drawings are exceptional, and the book is worthy of purchase if only to add these drawings to a collection. Highly recommended for medium to large academic libraries, public libraries (in

Arkansas and neighboring areas), and for personal collections. (KLK)

Atlas of electroencephalography in the dog and cat. By Richard W. Redding and Charles E. Knecht. New York: Praeger; 1984. 387p. $39.95. ISBN 0-03-016929-7.

It seems unusual that although the application of electroencephalography, or EEG, is widespread in human medicine, its use in veterinary medicine has been rather limited. The aim of this text is to teach the basic techniques of electroencephalography, and then it provides more than 150 sample EEGs of various breeds of dogs and cats. The first group of artifacts concentrates on breed and species differences, the rest concentrates on characteristic EEGs based on organic, inorganic, and neurological stimuli. For each artifact, however, the species, age, and sex of the animal, medical history and signs, an EEG description and sedation are listed. The index needs better cross-referencing, e.g., you can find "Arabian Horse," but not "Horse," or even "Horse, Arabian." Redding and Knecht are both diplomates of the American College of Veterinary Medicine (Neurology), an association founded in 1972 that is devoted to increasing the competence of practicing vets. A further note: this book is printed on acid-free paper. Recommended for veterinary medicine collections, both academic and private. (KLK)

Attitudes and behavior; an annotated bibliography. By Daniel J. Canary and David R. Seibold. New York: Praeger; 1984. 221p. $22.95. ISBN 0-03-060293-9.

> In compiling this bibliography, the authors had four main goals in mind: (1) provision of a current and broad-based bibliography of papers dealing with metatheoretical, theoretical, methodological, or applied aspects of attitude-behavior relationships; (2) reflection of the multidisciplinary nature of scholarly work on attitudes and actions; (3) identification of areas of commonality; and (4) to aid both students and experts in the field. Included in the scope of this work, in addition to attitude-behavior research, is literature concerned with identifying and explaining the determinants of action. The annotations are restricted to published papers; not included are dissertations, textbooks, and papers giving cursory treatment of the subject. Emphasis is placed on papers published since 1969. A coding scheme has used to characterize each article according to type and purpose of paper, procedures employed, moderating factors, and strength of the attitude-behavior relation. (BAL)

Biographical dictionary of psychology. By Leonard Zusne. Westport, CT: Greenwood Press; 1984. 563p. $49.95. ISBN 0-313-24027-2.

> First published in 1975 as *Names in history of psychology,* this volume presents short biographies of deceased psychologists and persons from other fields who contributed to the development of psychology. This version includes most of the original entries plus 101 new names, covering the field through 1982. Entries list specific contributions, main points of theoretical contributions, philosophies held, inventions and discoveries made, methodologies initiated, books and seminal articles written, research conducted, laboratories, journals and institutions founded, and major influence. Standard biographical information is also included. Each entry provides a list of references to further biographies. The material is organized alphabetically. Appendices include a chronological listing by birth date, rank order or relative standing in comparison with

the other entries, and a geographical/chronological list of institutions and individuals. (BAL)

Butterflies east of the great plains. By Paul A. Opler and George O. Krizek. Baltimore: Johns Hopkins University Press; 1984. 294p. $49.50. ISBN 0-8018-2938-0.

Not your average field guide, Opler and Krizek have paid more attention here to the behavior, population structure, and ecological considerations of butterflies than to distribution, identification, and variation. Nearly 400 butterflies are described in rather technical terms, and 54 color plates offer 324 striking photographs, differentiating between the male and female specimens in many cases. The 30-page introductory chapter discusses the natural history of butterflies, but it is accompanied by 36 murky black and white photos. Included is a 355-item bibliography, a very short glossary, and indexes. Recommended for academic libraries and large public libraries with serious butterfly aficionados. (KLK)

(A) Dictionary of drug abuse terms and terminology. By Ernest L. Abel. Westport, CT: Greenwood Press, 1984. 187p. $29.95. ISBN 0-313-24095-7.

An updated version of the author's *Marihuana dictionary,* this work contains words and expressions dealing with the use of drugs likely to be abused. Common terms, technical terms, and slang terms are all included. Definitions are usually one sentence or less, with longer definitions for a few entries. Terms relating to tobacco and alcohol are excluded due to the large number relating to each substance. Because of the constantly changing drug subculture, the language of drug abuse changes very rapidly. Thus, although this dictionary is extensive in coverage it is by no means exhaustive. It is, however, a very useful source in determining the meaning of current *and* past drug terminology. (DAT)

Dictionary of the life sciences. 2d ed., rev. Edited by E.A. Martin. New York: Pica Press; 1984. 396p. $25.00. ISBN 0-87663-740-3.

> Approximately 300 new entries have been added to this revised edition, the first edition having been published in 1976. The new entries represent recent advances in genetics, molecular biology, microbiology, and immunology. Original entries in these areas have been revised and updated, while coverage of classical zoology and botany has been reduced somewhat. Definitions, for the most part, are short, with a few accompanied by illustrations. Cross-references are used where appropriate. (BAL)

English-Russian dictionary of agriculture. Edited by I. Vaskhnil and others. New York: Pergamon; 1985. 876p. $40.00. ISBN 0-08-030784-1.

> This dictionary is the western version of a work originally published in the Soviet Union. It contains a comprehensive collection of English language agricultural terms with their Russian counterparts and was originally intended for the use of Russian scientists studying western literature. All areas of agricultural economics, veterinary science, agricultural engineering, plant breeding, conservation measures, and tropical agriculture. Entries are arranged in the alphabetical-class system, with the major terms arranged alphabetically and all terms containing the major term are listed as a subclass of that term. Thus, "shock" is listed in the main alphabet, but "cold shock" falls underneath the term "shock". The major drawback for English language users of this dictionary is that it only provides Russian definitions for English terms; it does not have a Russian-English translation. Although it is the most comprehensive English-Russian agricultural dictionary in existence, until a Russian-English volume appears it will probably have little use in North American libraries. (DAT)

(The) Facts on File dictionary of botany. Edited by Stephen Blackmore and Elizabeth Tootill. New York: Facts on File; 1984. 390p. $21.95. ISBN 0-87196-861-4.

> Over 3,000 entries cover the fields of pure and applied plant science, and include taxonomy and classification, anatomy and morphology, physiology, biochemistry, cell biology, plant pathology, genetics, evolution, and ecology. Selected terms in agricultural botany, horticulture, microbiology, laboratory techniques, and equipment are also included. Bacteria and viruses are covered as they relate to plant ecology and pathology. Definitions, for the most part, are concise and readable. Many are accompanied by helpful illustrations. Named plant species and genera are considered outside the scope, although divisions, classes and important orders have been included. Entries are organized alphabetically. Extensive cross-references guide users to other entries with relevant information and to synonyms. This dictionary is intended for use by students, naturalists, geographers, and just about anyone else interested in plants. (BAL)

(The) Giant handbook of food preserving basics. By Elizabeth and Robert Williams. Blue Ridge Summit, PA: TAB; 1984. 214p. $17.95. ISBN 0-8306-0727-7.

> A very practical work on how to grow, preserve, and even eat foods which may be enjoyed well out of season. The cost effectiveness of these activities is not ignored. Includes a collection of excellent photographs. Best for personal purchase and public libraries, large and small. (RGK)

(The) Handbook of environmental chemistry. Vol. 2, Part C: Reactions and processes. Edited by Otto Hutziner. New York: Springer-Verlag; 1985. 145p. $36.00. ISBN 0-387-13819-6.

> This work (at once both a handbook and a graduate level text) concludes Volume 2 of the three volume set. Concern is with physical factors (transport, adsorption) and chemical, photochemical and biochemical reactions in the environment and is reflected in the four extensive contributions. For most comprehensive chemistry collections as well as those on geology and meteorology. (RGK)

Handbook of ozone technology and applications. Vol. II: Ozone for drinking water treatment. Edited by Rip G. Rice and Sharan Netzer. Stoneham, MA: Butterworth; 1984. 378p. $59.95. ISBN 0-250-40577-6(v.2).

> This volume of the handbook series concerns the application of ozone for the treatment of drinking water. Great emphasis is given ozone's powerful disinfectant and oxidant properties with the added advantage of the non-production of undesirable by-products. European sources have been heavily drawn upon for this work since that is where most of the experience has been. Over one-third of the volume is devoted to a bibliography of some 1600 citations (in addition to 260 as chapter references). A good possibility for municipal and other government libraries as well as industrial special libraries with an interest in the uses of ozone. (RGK)

How to find out in psychology; a guide to the literature and methods of research. By D.H. Borchardt and R.D. Francis. Oxford; New York: Pergamon Press; 1984. 189p. $29.50. ISBN 0-08-031280-2.

> The stated purpose of this volume is to guide psychology students towards documented information and to suggest sources leading to recorded data and their use. In addition, it attempts to aid students with research methodology and the presentation of the results of psychological research. The book is divided into eleven chapters and covers the following areas: definitions and overviews of psychology, historical and theoretical works, bibliographic aids (including computer searches), sources for special fields of psychology, preparation for research, citations and card files, principles and methods of research, and various professional concerns. The sources that are listed are annotated and serve to clarify psychology as a discipline. While it does not provide a comprehensive list, the sources selected for inclusion are regarded as authoritative and/or basic to the study of psychology. The bibliography provided in an appendix could serve as a useful checklist in evaluating the holdings of a psychology library. This book also does a nice job of explaining the Dewey Decimal and Library of Congress classification systems. (BAL)

Illustrated encyclopedia of human histology. By R.V. Krstić. New York: Springer-Verlag; 1984. 450p. $38.50. ISBN 0-387-13142-6.

> This volume addresses new developments in the field of histology by providing concise definitions complemented by over 1500 figures. The entries, brief in length, strive to be as elementary as possible. Written in the style of encyclopedias, the author has attempted to illustrate fundamental histological terms, list synonyms, and describe morpho-functional phenomena. Latin terms are included where appropriate. Many of the entries are followed by a list of suggested readings. Cross-references for synonyms or related terms are used generously. Figures include halftones, pen drawings, and diagrams. As a reference tool, this book should prove valuable to everyone from the beginning student to the advanced researcher. (BAL)

International directory of contract laboratories. Compiled by Edward M. Jackson. New York: Dekker; 1985. 157p. $59.50. ISBN 0-8247-7415-9.

> The focus of this directory is *exclusively* on commercial and contract laboratories as a service to the toxicology community. Unique to this tool are laboratory listings which conduct testing on both ingredients and consumer products. Almost 100 United States locations are cited and over a dozen elsewhere. This work is also published as Vol. 3 No. 2 of *Cutaneous and ocular toxicology.* (RGK)

Nutrients in foods. By Gilbert A. Leveille and others. Cambridge, MA: The Nutrition Guild; 1983. 291p. $29.95. ISBN 0-938550-00-4.

> *Nutrients in Foods* presents the nutrient composition of more than 2700 foods showing almost all of the dietary nutrient factors known to be essential for the growth and maintenance of human beings. For each food item, data from thirty-two different categories are provided, including macronutrients, vitamins, minerals, electrolytes, and trace minerals. Entries are arranged alphabetically under a broad food classification, such as crackers, and are listed by brand or type under each category. All of the information is taken from the Michigan State University Nutrient Data Bank and has been updated as of 1982. A number of food manufacturers have contributed to this database, and entries for different foods will often have information pertaining to specific brand names as well as generic or homemade equivalents. This book should be a useful supplement to the *Composition of Foods* tables published by the U.S. Department of Agriculture. (DAT)

Psychological testing and assessment of the mentally retarded; a handbook. By Manny Sternlicht and Lillian Martinez. New York: Garland Publishing; 1985. 242p. $48.00. ISBN 0-8240-8905-7. (Developmental disabilities; v. 2.) (Garland reference library of social science; v. 261.)

> This handbook consists of an annotated bibliography of the literature addressing assessment and evaluation of the mentally retarded. Three main themes that are present regard assessment of innate abilities and handicaps; determining the success of previous education and training; and personality factors. The initial introductory chapter presents trends in psychological testing and evaluation of the mentally retarded, along with past and present developments. Thereafter, the bibliography is divided into nine chapters covering measurement of intelligence, assessment of cognitive and adaptive behaviors, educational achievement, personality, organic damage, measurement of social characteristics, psychomotor abilities, vocational competencies, and informal observational procedures. An appendix lists primary references, not annotated, for major assessment instruments. An author index is also included. (BAL)

Spiders of the world. By Rod and Ken Preston-Mafham. New York: Facts on File Publications; 1984. 191p. $17.95. ISBN 0-87196-996-3.

> The authors share a real fondness for spiders, and it shows throughout this valuable book. Generously illustrated, primarily with color photographs taken by the authors, the prose is entertaining and informative. Various components of spiders' "lifestyles" are described in general terms, but specific details and examples are plentiful. Because this book grew out of years of lectures given to the public, care has been taken in the preparation of the glossary and guide to further reading. A good choice for almost any library, it is especially suited for undergraduate collections and public libraries, perhaps even for personal collections. (KLK)

Tests; a comprehensive reference for assessments in psychology, education and business. Supplement. Edited by Richard C. Sweetland and Daniel J. Keyser. Kansas City, MO: Test Corporation of America; 1984. 426p. $65.00. ISBN 0-9611286-4-X (lib. bdg.)

> As a supplement to the original volume, *Tests,* published in 1983 (reviewed in this issue of *STL*), the work contains reference to over 500 new tests and some older tests excluded from the previous edition. The Supplement and original volume are to be used together as quick reference guides to nearly 4,000 English language tests for psychologists, educators, and human resource personnel. The format remains the same with statements of purpose, description, cost, availability, and publisher given for each test. One new feature in the present volume is an appendix entitled Selected Test Illustrations which includes test elements published or revised since 1980. These illustrations amount to specimen pages or photographs of test equipment. The indexes for publishers, test titles, author, scoring service, and visually impaired tests are cumulative, thereby easing the task of identifying needed entries. (BAL)

(The) University of California/Sotheby book of California wine. Edited by Doris Muscatine and others. Berkeley: University of California Press/Sotheby Publications; 1984, 615p., $65.00. ISBN 0-520-05085-1.

> At first glance, 44 authors contributing 53 articles totalling 615 pages about California wine may seem a bit extravagant, if not overdone, but don't give up. Once you have read the preface by M.F.K. Fisher entitled, "Wine is Life," a gem all by itself, you are hooked. If some facet of California wine-making has been overlooked, this reviewer cannot imagine what it could be. From the early days of wine-making in eighteenth century California missions to modern viniculture, these lively essays bring new life to a popular topic. An extensive glossary (more than 300 terms) and a selectively annotated bibliography add to the book's usefulness. The two page colophon attests to the book's physical beauty. This un-

usual work, fruit of an even more unusual union (Sotheby's and the University of California) is a must for any enophile, and any library developing a complete collection in enology. While the price may be a bit high for smaller public libraries, it is well worth the expense for larger public and academic libraries. (KLK)

(The) World of venomous animals. By Marcos Freiberg and Jerry G. Walls. Neptune City, NJ: T.F.H. Publications; 1984. 191p. $19.95. ISBN 0-87666-567-9.

From jellyfish to cobras to the platypus, this is a rather cursory treatment of venomous animals. Although nearly 200 genera and species are mentioned, none are described in great detail: physical description, habitat, etc., and the symptoms and treatment of wounds are briefly discussed. The book is well illustrated with high quality color photos. Not an essential purchase, this overview will be of most value to undergraduate collections and also for public and school libraries. (KLK)

PHYSICAL SCIENCES

Chronology of eclipses and comets: AD 1-1000. Compiled by D. Justin Shove in collaboration with Alan Fletcher. Dover, NH: Boydell & Brewer Ltd.; 1985. 356p. $29.50. ISBN 0-85115-406-9.

An extremely comprehensive and scholarly study of the dates in the first ten centuries when eclipses and comets were observed throughout the world. Computers have been used to determine these events, then extant records that have been discovered by scholars are cited and analyzed. Reasons for errors in written records are discussed. Data include European, Mayan and Chinese documents. Presents an interesting collaboration of historians and astronomers. (EM)

Dictionary of organometallic compounds. New York: Chapman and Hall; 1984. 3232p. in 3 volumes. $990. ISBN 0-412-24710-0.

> This massive undertaking is a companion set to the *Dictionary of organic compounds,* now in its fifth edition. The two sets are similarly arranged and both are updated with annual supplements. The first two volumes are arranged in sections by element (except for those elements that do not form organometallic compounds or form compounds not well characterized, such as the noble gases). Organometallic compounds of each element are characterized as a class, then a list of general references follows. A graphic structural index allows for easy browsing of compounds, and then the main entries of the compounds begin. Besides giving the physical data for each compound, the primary literature through mid-1983 is included. The third volume contains a name index, molecular formula index, and an index to *Chemical Abstracts* registry numbers. It is very apparent that a great deal of time and effort has gone into this work. Although undergraduates will make use of this, researchers will find it most helpful. An essential purchase for academic chemistry collections supporting graduate programs plus industrial special libraries. (KLK).

Earth and astronomical sciences research centres: a world directory of organizations and programmes. Edited by Jennifer M. Fitch. Essex, UK: Longman; 1984. 742p. $200.00. ISBN 0-582-90020-4. (Distributed by Gale Research.)

> This directory provides details on some 3,500 industrial, governmental, academic organizations, laboratories, and observatories located in over 130 countries. Earth sciences has been combined with astronomical sciences for both are involved in remote sensing techniques. The arrangement is geographic and within the national sections organizations are listed alphabetically. Included too are senior scientists, expenditures, activities, and publications. Where appropriate translations (not transliterations) are provided. There is an index of titles of establishments and a very complete subject index. For all science collections in industry, academe, and the larger public libraries. (RGK)

Electronic ready reference manual. By Edward Pasahow. New York: McGraw-Hill; 1985. 565p. $24.50. ISBN 0-07-048723-5.

> Provides a single source of current electronics information for engineers and technicians. Note that space is *not* devoted to pages of trigonometric and logarithmic tables. Common usage of pocket calculators is assumed. Vital for quick reference service in any physical science collection or as a personal purchase. The author is a design and development engineer with many publications to his credit. (RGK)

Lange's handbook of chemistry. 13th ed. Edited by John A. Dean. New York: McGraw-Hill; 1985. 1960p. $57.00. ISBN 0-07-016192-5.

> Although a great deal of this standard reference book remains relatively unchanged, there are some differences worth noting. Only those of us who have agonized over a slide rule can truly appreciate the wonder we call "the table of logarithmic functions." Alas, this table, along with the table of trigonometric functions, has been left out of this edition, due in toto to the "ubiquitous hand calculator." The organic chemistry section, easily the largest in the book, has been completely revised, incorporating the 1979 IUPAC rules for nomenclature, replacing the system prescribed by *Chemical Abstracts.* The data provided for the 7600 organic compounds are about the same with the addition of flash point data. The tables for organic acids feature expanded pK_a values, and the thermodynamic tables for the alkali family have been revised to include updated information. New to this edition is a variety of carbon-13 NMR data, reflecting the importance of an expanding field in chemistry. Recommended for all academic industrial and public libraries with large science collections. (KLK)

Line coincidence tables for inductively coupled plasma atomic emission spectrometry. Two volumes. 2d ed. By P. W. J. M. Boumans. New York: Pergamon; 1984. Mixed pagination. $215.00/set. ISBN 0-08-03404-X.

A somewhat massive collection of 896 "coincidence tables" which now in its second edition has become a "bible" for spectroscopists but will require constant updating at least twice a decade (the first edition came out in 1980). This set encourages this need and possibility by using punched sheets held in place by large removeable screws (as opposed to the undesirable loose-leaf format). For collections on plasma spectroscopy. Compiler is with Phillips Research Laboratories, Eindhoven, The Netherlands. (RGK)

Radiation technology handbook. By Richard Bradley. New York: Dekker; 1984. 334p. $59.75. ISBN 0-8247-7217-2.

Serves the dual purpose of a handbook for workers in several fields and a relatively simple test for students of industrial radiation technology. Coverage includes physical aspects of radiation, safety, irradiated polymers, and a wide variety of applications. The glossary is extensive and well-chosen. Primarily for physical science collections. Author is with E. R. Squibb, East Brunswick, NJ. (RGK)

SCIENCE, GENERAL

Apple Lisa: a user-friendly handbook. By Joseph Coleman. Blue Ridge Summit, PA: TAB; 1984. 308p. $24.95. ISBN 0-8306-0691-2.

One of TAB's useful, easy-to-follow books, this is a paean to the Apple Lisa. The author, who has written several technical books, obviously prefers Lisa to IBM's Personal Computer. From purchase to storage, he feels this is the easiest and most useful computer available. Features exercises, many relevant diagrams and charts and very clear exposition. For public libraries and for personal purchase. (RGK)

(The) Beginnings of the Nobel Institution: The science prizes, 1901-1915. By Elisabeth Crawford. New York: Cambridge University Press; 1984. 281p. $34.50. ISBN 0-521-26584-3.

As a unique work, this one deserves reference status in libraries serving the scientific community worldwide. Included are details on the prehistory of the "institution", the internal or private history, and finally its public face or interactions with the public and the scientific community. Extensive appendices provide historic data in areas such as Nobel's will, his foundation's statutes, committee members, and prize-winners in physics and chemistry, 1901-1915. The author is with the Centre National de la Recherche Scientifique Groupe d'Etudes et de Recherches sur la Science, Paris. (RGK)

Bowker 1985 complete sourcebook of personal computing. New York: Bowker; 1984. 1050p. $19.95(paper). ISBN 0-8352-1931-3.

This rather massive (and necessarily so) guide is based on available information on microcomputers and on any product or organization related to such computers. Includes listings of hardware, software, peripheral hardware products (e.g., disk drives), magazines (over 550 currently available), user groups (some 1770 arranged by application, geography, and finally profiles), and even other books and directories (including Bowker's competition). The index appears scant but is indeed comprehensive and well-organized for quick use. This compilation is updated and expanded considerably over the 1984 edition which means that personal computer aficionados will be well-advised to consider the consultation (or purchase) of the most recent volume to keep up-to-date. And the purchase price (at last for 1985) encourages such acquisitions. (RGK)

Dictionary of computing and new information technology. Compiled by A. J. Meadows and others. 2d ed. New York: Nichols; 1984. 229p. $29.50. ISBN 0-85038-370-8.

> Described as a "self-standing" dictionary, almost 5000 terms are included to cover the bulk of computer jargon as it exists today. For any collection on the subject as well as for librarians and engineers wishing to extend their backgrounds. (RGK)

(The) Master handbook of high-level microcomputer lanuages. By Charles F. Taylor. Blue Ridge Summit, PA: TAB; 1984. 359p. $21.95. ISBN 0-8306-0733-1.

> This work is about computer languages, specifically high-level ones that are available for use on microcomputers, and the descriptions are based according to the point of view of the user. Emphasis is on features of each of ten languages that are common to most implementations. Machine-dependent features such as graphics are ignored (except for Logo). For computer science collections in community colleges, public libraries, and for personal purchase. (RGK)

Science and technology in China. By Tong B. Tang. London: Longman; 1984. 269p. (Longman guide to world science and technology; vol. 3.) $85.00. ISBN 0-582-90056-5. (Dist. by Gale)

> After an introductory chapter about China, other chapters cover the social aspect of life there in regard to science, followed by chapters devoted to specific disciplines, such as biomedical topics, agriculture, earth science, mineral industries, energy and transportation. A separate chapter on science and technology in Taiwan completes the book. Appendixes cover statistics, five-year plans and a directory of major research establishments. There is a subject index and an index of organizations. Emphasizes work sponsored by the government and by academic institutions. Provides a thorough discussion of the subject. (EM)

(The) Software handbook. By Dimitris N. Chorafas. Princeton, NJ: Petrocelli; 1984. 461p. $49.95. ISBN 0-89433-248-1.

>A somewhat unique presentation to help in the exploitation of computers and communications (e.g., by encouraging their limits) through a better analysis of the job under consideration and what it entails. The work is written in a direct manner (seemingly without jargon) and with very specific examples. Primarily for the computer professional who needs guidance in areas such as project management and the art of program administration, two of four major areas attacked. Can be used for quick reference or long-term study. Author affiliation not given. (RGK)

University science and engineering libraries. 2d ed. By Ellis Mount. Westport, CT: Greenwood; 1985. 303p. $35.00. ISBN 0-313-23949-5.

>During the ten years since the first edition of this text, the number of changes, improvements, and developments in and among university science and engineering libraries certainly has validated the need for this extensive revision. The choices of the fifteen American universities and colleges plus one in Canada used in the survey of facilities, services, and staff were excellent. The data gleaned formed a solid basis for the discourse and makes this indeed a truly worthy contribution to the literature of librarianship. Of considerable and obvious value is the currency of the well-chosen chapter references, the strong section on management of libraries (which includes up-to-date pieces on computers and networking), and the clear library layout figures (though unhappily rather few in number). Dr. Mount writes rather succinctly and pedagogically (as he is a well-known instructor of library services). The work is definitely aimed primarily at the inexperienced library service student who may only barely have heard of these kinds of university operations. Happily though this is also excellent fodder for graduate university and college librarians who may wish to consider the report as a state-of-the-art presentation. The author is an Assistant Professor at the School of Library Service, Columbia University. (RGK)

Who's who in science in Europe: a biographical guide in science, technology, agriculture, and medicine. 4th ed. London: Longmans; 1984. 3 vols. $500.00. ISBN 0-582-90109-X. (Dist. by Gale)

> The first updating since 1978, this set of three volumes contains more than 2,500 pages and lists over 30,000 scientists. Thus it offers a thorough coverage of those scientists located in 30 countries of eastern and western Europe (excluding the USSR). Science is defined as consisting of the natural and physical sciences, engineering, agriculture and medicine. Following the alphabetical listing of biographical sketches, there is a section arranged by countries which lists scientists under one of eight categories of science, as chosen by the scientists themselves. Covers those employed in government, industry, educational institutions and also elected members of national science academies. Sketches provide the usual information as well as a listing of publications for the persons including such data. A very complete listing. (EM)

EXTANT

Annual reports on the progress of chemistry. Vol. 80, 1983. Section B: Organic chemistry. London: The Royal Society of Chemistry; 1984. 403p. $114.50. ISBN 0-85186-151-2.

> Progress in the area of organic chemistry during 1983 is represented by a review of the literature made available from 2082 citations for that year. Of special interest, and appearing for the first time in this series, is a report on "host-guest chemistry" (involving chemicals such as crown ethers and clathrates). For any serious organic chemistry collection. (RGK)

Astronomy and astrophysics abstracts. Vol. 37: Literature 1984, Part 1. Edited by S. Böhme and others. New York: Springer-Verlag; 1984. 937p. $53.10. ISBN 0-387-13937-0.

> This continuation volume records literature published in 1984 and received before August 15, 1984 (hence the Part I designation). The set is devoted to all aspects of astronomy, astrophysics, and their border fields. It is the crème de la crème abstracting tool for the subject fields involved and is still a subscription price bargain. For all serious physical science libraries. (RGK)

Carbohydrate chemistry. Vol. 16, Part I: Mono-, di-, and trisaccharides and their derivatives. Senior reporter is N. R. Williams. London: The Royal Society of Chemistry; 1984. 286p. $72.00. ISBN 0-85186-162-8.

> A review of the literature published on carbohydrate chemistry during 1982 (available by February 1983). A total of 1393 citations are recorded. For all comprehensive chemistry collections. (RGK)

Comprehensive treatise of electrochemistry. Vol. 9. Electrodics: experimental techniques. Edited by Ernest Yeager and others. New York: Plenum; 1984. 451p. $65.00. ISBN 0-306-41570-4.

> As a series, this treatise provides mature statements about the present positions in electrochemical methodology. This particular volume covers the more traditional methods for the study of electrochemical interfaces and the kinetics of processes occurring at such interfaces. Though not a quick-use reference tool, it is a set of volumes which deserves a front-row place in serious physical science collections in academe and industry. (RGK)

Encyclopedia of chemical processing and design. Vol. 22: Fire extinguishing chemicals to fluid flow, slurry systems and pipelines. Edited by John J. McKetta and William A. Cunningham. New York: Dekker; 1985. 419p. $115.00. ISBN 0-8247-2472-0(v. 22).

>Continues a noble series with well-written coverage from "fire extinguishing chemicals" to "fluid flow, slurry systems and pipelines" involving a total of 22 topics. Apart from striking exceptions, such as "flocculation" with 127 references, the contributions in general provide only scant literature citations and with currency not too obvious. Nevertheless (and despite a high cost), the series must receive prime acquisition consideration for most engineering collections. (RGK)

Organic electronic spectral data. Vol. XX (1978). Edited by John C. Phillips and others. New York: Wiley; 1984. 1040p. $120.00. ISBN 0-471-81808-9.

>The data in this volume of the series were abstracted from 96 journals covering the year 1978 *only*. There are some 20,000 entries. About 450,000 spectra are included in all 20 volumes published so far. (RGK)

Organic reactions. Vol. 32. Edited by William G. Dauben and others. New York: Wiley; 1984. 533p. $54.95. ISBN 0-471-88101-5.

>In this series continuation only two synthetic chemical reactions are discussed, and they in the consummate detail that is usual for volumes in this reference tool. Included are extensive tables of (hopefully) all known examples of the reaction along with the citations gleaned from exhaustive literature searches. For all serious reference collections on organic chemistry. (RGK)

SCI-TECH ONLINE

Ellen Nagle, Editor

DATABASE NEWS

Biotechnology Database Announced

BIOBUSINESS is available from DIALOG as a source of current information on the business applications of biological and biomedical research. Tailored to the needs of business decision-makers, the database covers both business and life science literature on laboratory and clinical research that has commercial importance. Over 1,000 publications, including journal articles, short research communications, review articles, and meeting literature are monitored for topics relevant to *BIOBUSINESS*. The file is the result of a joint effort between BIOSIS, producer of *BIOSIS PREVIEWS* and Information Access Company, producer of *Management Contents*. References are selected from both of these databases, and unique subject indexing is added to create *BIOBUSINESS*.

Four broad subject areas are covered in the database:

1. Agriculture, which includes crop production studies that have potential economic impact; methods to increase crop yield; crop pests and their control; agronomic and horticultural crops; forestry studies; production, feeding, breeding, and diseases of domestic animals; and veterinary medicine as it applies to domestic animals.
2. Biotechnology, which includes genetic engineering; protein production; biomass conversion; waste treatment; studies of pollution, conservation, and resource renewal; new medical diagnostics, instrumentation, prosthetics, and implants; and industrial health.

3. Food and Beverages, which includes food technology studies, industrial microbiology, fermentation, and food packaging and processing.
4. Pharmaceuticals, which includes studies of the manufacturing of drugs, packaging, new drugs, new uses for drugs, toxicity studies, new drug delivery systems, natural products that have potential pharmacological use, and toxicology of cosmetics.

BIOBUSINESS concentrates in a single database the information needed to help predict which areas of biological research have the most potential for commercial growth. Business executives, financial analysts, and product and marketing professionals can evaluate possible economic impacts resulting from new developments in biotechnology. The file can also be used to review the business applications of existing life science technologies. The references in *BIOBUSINESS* will be of special interest to those involved in agriculture and forestry, genetic engineering, food technology, and the production and development of pharmaceutical products, and other industries affected by breakthroughs in biology and biomedicine.

BIOBUSINESS records feature detailed data on the subject, source, and author(s) of the original reference, and for about 76% of the records, a descriptive abstract. Subject indexing consists of controlled subject headings and subject codes developed especially for the new file and natural language descriptors that help to enrich and clarify an article's title. The subject codes are particularly useful for quick and accurate retrieval on broad biological and biomedical topics such as pharmacology, agronomy, or industrial microbiology. Company names and personal names mentioned in an article are also searchable.

Available as File 285, *BIOBUSINESS* contains approximately 16,000 records dating from the beginning of 1985. It will be updated monthly with about 2,000 records per update. The file will be available on both DIALOG systems. The price for searching is $117 per connect hour, $.25 per full record printed online and $.35 per full record printed offline.

Aerospace Database Online

DIALOG is now offering *Aerospace Database,* co-produced by the American Institute of Aeronautics and Astronautics/Technical Information Service and the National Aeronautics and Space Administration/Scientific and Technical Information Branch. Available as File 108, the database corresponds to two printed publications: *International Aerospace Abstracts* (IAA) and *Scientific and Technical Aerospace Reports* (STAR). The file provides worldwide coverage of sci-tech literature from over 1600 periodicals, as well as from conferences, books, theses, and unpublished report literature. Approximately 50% of the documents originate outside the United States.

Aerospace Database is an "unparalleled source for information on technological innovation", according to DIALOG. The database encompasses a broad range of aerospace disciplines, including: atmospheric and space sciences; aerodynamics; aircraft and aerospace systems; communications and navigation; propulsion; energy production and conversion; structural engineering and analysis; advanced materials; and laser and robotic technologies. In addition, the file contains extensive coverage of chemistry, geosciences, electronics, environmental studies, computer sciences, and relevant social, economic, and legal issues. Research and development from over 40 countries, including a substantial amount of material from Communist-bloc countries, China, and Japan is incorporated in the file. Approximately 90% of the records include abstracts. Subject indexing consists of descriptors from the *NASA Thesaurus,* IAA and STAR subject classifications and codes, and, for a small portion of the file, COSATI (Committee on Scientific and Technical Information) classifications and codes.

The file began with approximately 75,000 records entered from 1984 forward. Earlier portions of the file will be available on DIALOG in the future; semimonthly updates will add approximately 2500 records. The price for searching File 108 is $78 per connect hour. Print costs are $.20 per full record printed online and $.25 per full record printed offline. The database is available on DIALOG Version 2 and on the original system. Access to, use of, or distribution of data contained in the *Aerospace Database* is limited to users within the United States and is intended only for organizations or persons whose primary activities are within the United States or its territories. Access by non-U.S. goverments, organizations, or persons acting on their behalf is not allowed without written approval of the American Institute of Aeronautics/Technical Information Service. Requests may be directed to: Technical Information Service, American Institute of Aeronautics and Astronautics, 555 West 57th Street, New York, NY 10019.

Drug Information Fulltext Enhanced

The 1985 *Drug Information Fulltext* file, available from BRS and DIALOG, has been updated and improved. The American Society of Hospital Pharmacists, producer of the database, has added coverage of 30 new drug monographs. More than 50% of the *American Hospital Formulary Service* monographs have been revised from the 1984 version; the "Penicillins" section of the *Formulary* is completely new. The database contains complete full-text evaluative monographs from both the *Formulary* and the *Handbook on Injectable Drugs*.

Cancerexpress Database Discontinued

The National Cancer Institute has discontinued the *Cancerexpress* database effective October 1, 1985. The database which served as a high quality journal current awareness file did not receive sufficient use to warrant remaining as a separate file. All records in *Cancerexpress* are also included in the National Library of Medicine's *Cancerlit* database, so the data will continue to be searchable and retrievable online.

SEARCH SYSTEM NEWS

Toxicology Data Network Announced

The Toxicology Information Program operated by the National Library of Medicine (NLM) has announced 2 databanks in the broad areas of toxicology, chemistry and hazardous waste information, as the first components of the Library's new Toxicology Data Network (TOXNET) data retrieval system. One file is an expanded version of the *Toxicology Data Bank* (*TDB*) currently online and retains the TDB name. The second file, known as the *Hazardous Substances Data Bank* (*HDSB*), is a broader, more comprehensive file initially containing the entire TDB content. Both of these files are maintained on a Data General Eclipse minicomputer and have been accessible to domestic MEDLARS users on the TOXNET system since July 1985. The TOXNET system will operate in parallel with NLM's ELHILL system under MEDLARS.

In the mid 1970's, the Toxicology Information Program initiated the development of a data retrieval file, known as the Toxicology Data Bank, to collect, organize and disseminate information about the effects of chemical substances on human health and biological systems. This original *TDB* file has experienced considerable growth since its first public availability in 1978; it is currently composed of approximately 4,000 chemical records containing referenced data statements. The file is peer-reviewed by an expert panel of toxicologists, the TDB Peer Review Committee.

Starting in the early 1980's, NLM's Specialized Information Services (SIS) set out to improve the building and searching of the *TDB* by: (a) streamlining the data entry and maintenance procedures used to build and update *TDB* records; (b) expanding the number and completeness of its chemical profiles; (c) increasing the permissible record length; (d) utilizing new computer technologies to aid the peer review process; and (e) improving the software to facilitate searching and retrieval. Through a collaborative program between SIS and the Information Technology Branch of the Library's Lister Hill Center, existing software was adapted to achieve these goals. The resultant system was named TOXNET. An event that proved to have a significant impact on the efforts to enrich *TDB* content and improve the support software was the passage of the Comprehensive Environmental Response, Compensation and Liability Act (CERCLA) of 1980, commonly called the Superfund Act. CERCLA authorized cleanup and emergency response for hazardous substances released into the environment, and the cleanup of inactive hazardous waste disposal sites. Section 104 (i) of the Act called for the "Establishment and Maintenance of an Inventory of Literature, Research, and Studies on the Health Effects of Toxic Substances." NLM was assigned a role within the Department of Health and Human Service's activities under the foregoing requirement. The Library identified its publicly available chemical and toxicological files as the basis for this Inventory. It also sought to expand these files, further improve computer capabilities for data record creation, and develop methods for providing rapid and effective access to the data.

The TOXNET system is a fully integrated software system with such modules as remote online data entry for the creation and maintenance of records; online interactive review and editing; electronic mail/messaging; in-process control/tracking for all records; and a new search and retrieval capability.

Initially, the Library had planned to offer *TDB* with the CERCLA-related enhancements on a single database, replacing the original *TDB*. For various reasons it was found preferable to offer two files, both to start with information on the same 4,100 chemicals. One is the NLM-supported *TDB* with 96 data elements; the other is the new *HSDB* with 144 data elements. The data elements (or fields) in both files are arranged in the following ten broad categories: substance identification; manufacturing/use information; chemical and physical properties; safety and handling; toxicity/biomedical effects; pharmacology; environmental fate/exposure potential; exposure standards and regulations; monitoring and analysis methods; and additional references. Users familiar with the ELHILL *TDB* should note that the TOXNET *TDB* will continue to focus upon toxicological information and maintain a high degree of quality control through review by a committee of experts. The scope of *HSDB* includes and expands upon that of the *TDB* by providing fuller information primarily in the areas of environmental fate and exposure, standards and regulations, monitoring and analysis, and safety and handling. Data are extracted not only from the materials on the *TDB* source list but also from a variety of other sources, including Government documents and special reports. This more comprehensive file (*HSDB*) will be scientifically reviewed and edited, but short of the detailed peer review of *TDB*. The new *TDB* and *HSDB* files will be priced comparable to the $75/hour average prime-time charge for the existing TDB.

TDB and *HSDB* are but the first two files on TOXNET. The acquisition of other toxicology and environmental files is being explored. Near-term possibilities according to NLM, include moving the National Institute for Occupational Safety and Health's *Registry of the Toxic Effects of Chemical Substances* (RTECS) from ELHILL to TOXNET, and mounting the National Cancer Institute's *Chemical Carcinogenesis Research and Information Systems* (CCRIS) and the Environmental Protection Agency's *Oil and Hazardous Materials Technical Assistance Documentation System* (OHM-TADS) databases.

A number of menus are being developed to facilitate searching for the novice user. These screens will guide users along each step of the way, allowing them to choose from a list of items they are interested in seeing. Neither prior MEDLARS training nor other computer experience will be necessary in order to search TOXNET effectively in this mode.

NLM is also offering a new, low-cost practice file called *INTRO-*

TOX for users of the TOXNET system. INTROTOX consists of a small subset of the *HSDB* file. The practice file permits users to familiarize themselves with the TOXNET system before undertaking searching in earnest on the *Toxicology Data Bank* (*TDB*) and the *Hazardous Substances Data Bank* (*HSDB*) at full cost. Only connect time will be charged to users while practicing in *INTROTOX* ($56.50/hour non-prime time and $60.25/hour prime time).

SCI-TECH IN REVIEW

Suzanne Fedunok, Editor

FOREIGN LANGUAGE BARRIER

van Bergeijk, Dies. Scientific and technical literature in foreign languages and library users. *International Association of Technological University Libraries Proceedings.* 17: 187-196; 1985.

The author, who is the director of the International Translations Center in Delft, Holland, makes a plea in this article for education of the user and of the librarian to the many tools available to get access to scientific and technical literature written in foreign languages. He also reviews these sources in general terms, emphasizing the publication of the *World Transindex.* He concludes with the remarks that "Librarians should know and advise clients where translations can be made, including the possibilities of production of machine translations in the (near) future. They should also know the disadvantages of such translations. Librarians who assist in carrying out literature searches should know which multilingual thesauri are available and where. They should know where existing scientific translations are available and how to obtain them expeditiously. Nowadays libraries and librarians have to cope with reduced resources, they have to find a balance between acquisitions and other services. The services which can be given should therefore by satisfactory." (7 refs.)

TRADITIONAL NONEMPIRICAL RESEARCH

Stephenson, Mary Sue. The research method used in subfields and the growth of published literature in those subfields: vertebrate paleontology and geochemistry. *Journal of the American Society for Information Science.* 36: 130-133; 1985 March.

The author is with the Graduate School of Library and Information Science of the University of Tennessee. In this paper she reports on a study of relationship between the method of research used in a scientific field (the independent variable) and the growth of literature in that field (as the dependent variable) to test the hypothesis that there is a significant correlation between the two. Earlier studies of how science progresses and grows centered on independent variables such as size of the scientific population, availability of outside funding, and stylistic considerations. In this study, an instrument was designed to assign quantitative values to published research, based on the method of research used. Two subfields of geology with varying growth rates, vertebrate paleontology and geochemistry, were selected for study, and in both cases the major hypothesis was proved. The author concludes that "as a result of this exploratory study several points can be made. First, the ability to apply this evaluative procedure at the level of the original article (as opposed to having to accumulate large amounts of retrospective secondary data such as citations) could provide a useful tool in reaching preliminary decisions regarding the potential growth patterns of new or changing subfields. Second, the results reported here may have implications for practitioners in fields which are either steady state or growing very slowly. The concept that researchers in a field that embraces a nonempirical research tradition may be, in effect, slowing down the growth of that field by their choice of method is worthy of further consideration." (15 refs.)

BOOK SELECTION USING COMPUTERS

Quinn, Kenneth. Using DIALOG as a book selection tool. *Library Acquisitions*. 9(1):79-82; 1985.

The writer is Science and Engineering Librarian at the University of Alabama at Huntsville. In this article he discusses his use of files such as MATHFILE, INSPEC, and CA SEARCH to make book selection decisions in the fields of mathematics, chemistry and computer science, with which he reports having only a rudimentary knowledge. The databases provided him with an up to date and comprehensive list of recently published monographs and proceedings. Some abstracts listed the contents of the books in question, while others such as MATHFILE, provided signed, critical reviews. The author gives the search statements used to generate such lists of titles in the different files studied. He concludes that "The searches could not have been duplicated manually, since the printed equivalents do not allow for selection by document type. The investment of money was considered very reasonable; not only was a comprehensive bibliography obtained, but many hours of time were saved." ( ) refs.)

SHORT CIRCUITS IN THE NETWORK

Somerfield, G. A. The future of the scientific journal. *Open.* 15: 137-143; 1983 March.

The author gives a model of the "information circle", or the information network operating in scientific research, and notes how new technologies such as word processing equipment, telecommunications networks, and the increasing use of databases, have influenced the processes. He describes "short circuits" caused in the circle by the dissemination virtually at random to unknown recipients of preprints, and believes that electronic mail will improve dissemination of this type of information, and goes on to suggest that use of an expert system would be preferable to electronic mail. The effect of the new technologies on publishers is explored with regard to quality control (refereeing and editorial standardization), production, marketing and distribution. He concludes that "no element in this network will remain static and drastic changes may occur in some. It will be a considerable time before a new state of equilibrium is reached, but the turmoil will be well worthwhile if the result is more efficient information transfer between scientists, engineers and managers leading to a better life for mankind." (4 refs.)

BIBLIOGRAPHIC INSTRUCTION FOR ENGINEERS

Vezier, Liliane. Ten years of turning out engineers for using scientific and technical information at the Compiegne University of Technology. *International Association of Technological University Libraries Proceedings.* 17: 151-152; 1985.

The author, who is a librarian at the university mentioned in the title, briefly describes her experience with a successful bibliographic instruction program designed to educate every engineer in the university to the existence of scientific and technical information, particularly of databases, and to where and when to use these information sources. Every half-year new students visit the library to receive a series of units of instruction. These sessions are followed up two years later by refresher courses and practice with databases. (0 refs.)

ONLINE CONTEXT OF RESEARCH

Piternick, Anne B. Traditional interpretation of "authorship" and "responsibility" in the description of scientific and technical documents. *Cataloging and Classification Quarterly*. 5: 17-33; 1985 Spring.

The author is a professor at the School of Librarianship at the University of British Columbia. This long and detailed article arose from several years of teaching a course on the creation of machine readable databases. To quote from her summary: "A study of printed abstracting services for scientific and technical documents shows divergences in the concepts of authorship and responsibility, and in the roles assigned to individuals and to organizations, arising primarily from the context in which the work discussed in a document was performed. The distinctions evident in the printed sources are becoming lost, especially through the processing of source data for online searching. . . . This then may be an appropriate time to examine the different approaches before the online revolution sweeps over us and existing distinctions are lost. . . . It is hoped that this study may prove interesting to those charged with retrospective searches of the literature. It may help to explain to the novice searcher why certain data elements now searchable online have never been regarded as important enough to index in print, and perhaps why some not indexed before the advent of automation may provide some insight into the importance of the context of research in influencing practices of description and indexing." (37 refs.)

USER SURVEY

Brember, V. L.; Leggate, P. Linking a medical user survey to management for library effectiveness. *Journal of Documentation*. 41: 1-14; 1985 March.

The authors are, respectively, affiliated with the Radcliffe Science Library and the Cairns Library of the John Radcliffe Hospital in Oxford, England. In this article they report on an intensive survey of users in the Oxford teaching hospitals and the University science departments using six survey techniques to investigate user's opinions, remembrance of past actions, immediate reporting of visits to the library, views of observers, and "the very specific view represented by individual events in the information seeking process." The results of each of these surveys are summarized, and the authors conclude that "the characteristic having most influence on information seeking behavior and library usage was the relative amounts of the user's time devoted to clinical practice and to research respectively. Three distinct user types were identified: the hospital or university researcher, the hospital practitioner, and the research-practitioner. The knowledge of the differences among members of the population to be served is essential to library effectiveness." (8 refs.)

ONE-WOMAN SHOW

Sliney, M. One-woman show: the case of the electronics library. *Aslib Proceedings*. 37: 207-212; 1985 April.

The author describes how she operated as an "OMB, or One-Man Band," in creating a small and efficiently run in-house library for an electronics company. Rather than contracting out the information services to a broker, she convinced her management and users of the cost-effectiveness of such a facility and set about to design it. Two problems found to be particularly troublesome were the sheer volume of trade literature and inadequate bibliographic control of data books and other specialist literature. (5 refs.)

SEARCHERS BEWARE

Roth, Dana Lincoln. The role of subject expertise in searching the chemical literature, and pitfalls that await the inexperienced searcher. *Database*. 8: 43-46; 1985 February.

In this article the author, who is the head of the Science and Engineering Libraries at Caltech, voices some concerns regarding various search services, the producers of indexes, and administrators of libraries. Inconsistent indexing, nomenclature variations, language, and transliterations problems are singled out as pitfalls. The author concludes that: "the current euphoria surrounding online's professionalizing influence must be viewed with some skepticism. The concept of the academic library or information center as the only or central resource for information services is basically unsound; both because of efforts by online services to deal directly with end-users and the fact that performance rather than qualifications is rapidly becoming the ground of acceptance. Search analysts with subject expertise will, almost by definition, deprofessionalize librarians who do not have a 'firm knowledge of the technologies and the disciplines that support information transfer, plus an application of this knowledge to a specific area', especially chemistry." (24 refs.)